D1506933

GATORS

*The
Inside Story of
Florida's
First SEC Title*

STEVE SPURRIER

with

NORM CARLSON

TRIBUNE
PUBLISHING
ORLANDO / 1992

For information:
Tribune Publishing
P.O. Box 1100
Orlando, Florida 32802

Tribune Publishing
Editorial Director: George C. Biggers III
Managing Editor: Dixie Tate Kasper
Senior Editor: Kathleen M. Kiely
Production Editor: Ken Paskman

Printed in the United States

First edition: October 1992
ISBN 0-941263-70-3

To the Gator family,
players, coaches, administration,
alumni and fans

In All Kinds of Weather,
We'll All Stick Together for
F-L-O-R-I-D-A

CONTENTS

ACKNOWLEDGMENTS VII

FOREWORD BY RAY GRAVES................................IX

1. SOME BASIC BELIEFS 1

2. FLORIDA: A COACH'S DREAM 11

3. A PASSING STYLE...17

4. FIVE CRUCIAL GAMES 25

5. LEARNING TO WIN 37

6. ROCKY TOP THRASHING................................45

7. AUBURN/GEORGIA ISN'T ONE GAME........51

8. GEORGIA COMES FIRST 59

9. OUR COACHING FAMILY 71

10. THE APPROACH TO 1991 83

11. BEATING A RESPECTED TEAM 93

12. SYRACUSE SLUMBER 103

13. BOUNCING BACK BIG 113

14. VICTORY OVER VOLS 123

15. WOUNDED WAR EAGLES 131

16. BRING ON THE DAWGS 141

17. 'THE DRIVE' WINS IT 149

18. SEC, FSU BOTH IMPORTANT 159

19. JERRI'S A STARR 171

20. SHANE MATTHEWS 175

21. Q&A 185

ABOUT THE AUTHORS 193

INDEX 201

ACKNOWLEDGMENTS

There wouldn't have been a championship to write a book about without the accomplishments of the players and coaches associated with the 1990 and 1991 University of Florida teams.

There wouldn't have been a road to the championship without the leadership of the senior classes the past two seasons. We were very fortunate to inherit quality young men like these.

And I would never have been in the position of writing books about coaching football without the faith and support of men who gave me opportunities.

Thanks to my college coach and good friend Ray Graves. Thanks to Doug Dickey, who gave me my first coaching job in 1978; to Pepper Rodgers, who hired me at Georgia Tech in 1979; and to Red Wilson, who gave an untested young coach a chance to install his own offense at Duke University from 1980 to 1982.

Special thanks to the late John Bassett, who took a gamble in giving me my first head coaching job with the Tampa Bay Bandits of the USFL in 1983.

This book probably wouldn't have been finished without the effort and patience of my secretary, Jan Hare, whose husband, Matt, watched the children while she typed and edited at the computer.

Many other patient and encouraging people helped Norm Carlson and me work through this project, most notably my wife, Jerri, and Norm's wife, Sylvia.

Thanks to Bruce Carden, Dixie Kasper, Kathleen M. Kiely and Ken Paskman for their detailed editing efforts on behalf of Tribune Publishing, our enthusiastic, cooperative publisher.

Finally, Rosemary Souder, our publishing consultant, is a true professional whose work and advice were tremendously helpful.

FOREWORD
BY RAY GRAVES

My brother Edwin, then the Postmaster of Knoxville, Tennessee, called me back in 1962 to tell me he had just seen a phenomenal high school quarterback play against my prep alma mater, Knoxville Central.

He said that this young man, Steve Spurrier of Science Hill High School in Johnson City, Tennessee, could punt, pass, run and kick field goals and extra points; and he was like a coach on the field, guiding his team with a self-assured confidence seldom seen in people his age.

My brother said this young man was almost too good to be true, and I should be recruiting him for the University of Florida. Well, we did recruit Steve, and to this day he is still almost too good to be true.

His father was a Presbyterian minister in Johnson City, and my father had also been a minister in East Tennessee. Perhaps as preacher's kids we had something in common, but for whatever reasons, Steve came to Florida, and I was fortunate to be his coach and a close personal friend for the past 30 years.

*Ray Graves is the winningest football coach
in the history of the University of Florida.
His teams were 70-31-4, a winning percentage of .686,
and they played in five bowl games, winning four of them.*

His accomplishments over the years, as an athlete and then as a coach, have not surprised me. Very early in our relationship I learned that he is a fierce competitor who thrives on pressure. When he gets that glint in his eye, that certain spark that true champions have, he rarely fails to achieve the goal he has at that moment.

Steve consistently produces the dramatic result under the glare of the spotlight. There are many instances that come to mind, but three of them stand out:

■ **The 1965 Florida-FSU game at Florida Field.** We were headed to the Sugar Bowl, and had never lost to FSU in Gainesville, but trailed 17-16 with 2:02 remaining and the ball at our 29-yard line.

Steve was standing next to me on the sideline during the kick-off while the coaching staff discussed strategy to move the ball close enough for a field goal attempt or, hopefully, a touchdown. Steve looked at me and calmly said, "Coach, don't worry about it, we'll score."

He went out there and completed three passes and ran for a five-yard gain to move the ball to the FSU 25-yard line in only 43 seconds. Then he rolled out to his right after noticing the FSU middle guard had jumped offside. Knowing he had a free play, he motioned Charlie Casey to go deep and hit him in dead stride for the winning touchdown.

■ **The 1966 Auburn game at Florida Field.** It was 27-27, and we were at the Auburn 23-yard line, fourth down and very long to go for a first down. Our unbeaten, untied season was on the line. We had an excellent placekicker in Wayne Barfield, but it was out of his range.

We called timeout to discuss what to do. Steve pointed to his chest and said, "I can make it, Coach, let me try." When the ball was placed on the tee, the laces were facing the kicker – the opposite of what you want – and he still kicked it right through for the victory.

■ **The 1966 Heisman Trophy presentation at the Downtown Athletic Club in New York City.** Steve had won the trophy that year over Bob Griese of Purdue by the biggest margin in history.

Following an outstanding response in his finest East Tennessee dialect, Steve called to the podium Dr. J. Wayne Reitz, president of the University of Florida, and presented the trophy to him, "because it belongs to the students, faculty and the university."

This was the first time any Heisman winner had ever turned his trophy over to his school. Now the Heisman committee presents two trophies, one to the winner and the other to his school.

As a player, and now as a coach, Steve has a confidence that he conveys to players, coaches and fans. He can think under pressure, which is a trait lacking in a lot of coaches. I truly believe that after they play the "Star Spangled Banner" and the game begins, having Steve Spurrier as our Gator head coach gives us an advantage over our opponent.

One of the best decisions I made as Director of Athletics was to bring Norm Carlson back home to the University of Florida as sports information director. He graduated from Florida in 1956, and I had known him when he was a rising young sportswriter with the *Atlanta Journal* in the late 1950s.

I had followed Norm's career as the sports information director at Auburn from 1959 to 1963, and he joined my staff in February of 1963. Steve entered school as a freshman the following September. They have been very good friends since, and there isn't anyone who could help Steve tell his story better than Norm, who has known and understood him so well for so many years.

Together they have produced an interesting book that provides insight into the philosophy and memories of an exceptionally bright football coach, one who quickly guided the Florida Gators to the top of the Southeastern Conference – Stephen Orr Spurrier.

RAY GRAVES
Athletic Director Emeritus,
University of Florida
Head Football Coach, 1960-69
Director of Athletics, 1960-79

GATORS

The Inside Story of Florida's First SEC Title

STEVE SPURRIER

with

NORM CARLSON

1

SOME BASIC BELIEFS

*You see things and you say,
"Why?" But I dream things
that never were; and I say,
"Why not?"*
– George Bernard Shaw

In the summer of 1991 I ran across that quote from George Bernard Shaw, which spelled out to me a basic belief that has helped guide my thinking.

This is the quotation I shared with our team several times early in 1991. I told them we were going to dream about things that never were, and we're asking: "Why not? Why not win the conference? Why not win seven games in the SEC? Why not win 10 games this season?"

Just because it has never happened at the University of Florida doesn't mean it can't. We won't look for reasons why Florida hasn't been successful or why we can't do this. We'll look for reasons why we can do it because there is no reason in the world why the Gators can't be successful in football. There is no reason in the world why the University of Florida shouldn't be at the very highest level of Division I college football.

I really believe that some of the problems Florida has experienced over the years are a result of our looking for reasons for our failure instead of saying, hey, there are no excuses.

1

That's what the coaching staff started telling our team as soon as I became the head coach: There are no excuses if we lose. We simply were not good enough, not tough enough or not smart enough – and that includes the coaches, too.

I firmly believe that if you think something is a problem, then it is a problem. If you view a situation – whatever it is – in a positive light, then everybody comes to believe that the situation is to our advantage.

One of the biggest problems we've had in the past – when we have not earned the success that we maybe were capable of – is we have made excuses and dwelled on what is negative. I'm a part of that as a player. Our teams were very close to success – one game away from winning the conference championship in both 1965 and 1966 – but we couldn't quite get it done.

I was part of that history as a player, and now I hope I'm part of changing it as a coach. Perhaps one day that will be my legacy as the head coach of the Gators.

I'm a big believer in using quotations from successful people. It's something I started back in 1983 with the Tampa Bay Bandits; it helped me and our players then, and it still does today.

"Preparation," "Persistence" and "Positive" are among the primary thoughts in my theory on what it takes to be successful. That's probably why so many of my favorite quotations relate to these themes.

It is important for a coach to give players something they can think about that makes sense. Give them something they can relate to that will be an incentive to train and prepare and to try to be the very best they can be. Hopefully, these thoughts will not only help them in their football careers, but in other facets of their lives as well.

One favorite quote is from General George Patton: "Most battles are won before they are ever fought."

I try to use this with our team during spring practice and when they are working out in the summer. The battles are usually won before the kickoff ever starts the game. The team that is the best prepared physically and mentally to play that day will usually win the game.

John Wooden, the brilliant UCLA basketball coach who won so many NCAA championships, says: "Failing to prepare is certainly preparing to fail." This is so true in life. Preparing to play the best we can each week is the cornerstone of our approach.

Then there is persistence. Teams and individuals who have this quality will succeed.

When I was at Duke in 1987 we lost a heartbreaking game to Maryland. We were ahead 22-7 with five minutes remaining in the game – Maryland had not done much of anything up to that point – and all of a sudden they made two long touchdown drives, went for two-point conversions twice successfully, and beat us 23-22.

It was an unbelievable loss, and afterward our locker room was like a funeral parlor. We had dominated the game, but had been forced to kick three field goals when we couldn't punch the ball in from the two-yard line.

I've never seen a bunch of coaches and players more depressed than that day at Maryland. When I got back to Durham, someone sent me some inspirational words used by former President Calvin Coolidge: "Nothing in the world can take the place of persistence. Talent will not; nothing is more common than unsuccessful men with talent. Genius will not; unrewarded genius is almost a proverb. Education will not; the world is full of educated derelicts. Persistence and determination are omnipotent, and the slogan 'Press On' has solved and always will solve the problems of the human race."

I told our guys that persistence and determination is all we have at the moment. There's no sense feeling sorry for ourselves. What happened is over, and maybe we'll learn from our lesson and go on from there. The next week we played a good Georgia Tech team in Durham, had our best game of the season and beat them 48-14.

In 1989, after we had beaten Clemson to start our six-game ACC winning streak, I ran across an excellent quote from the outstanding writer and physician Oliver Wendell Holmes: "I find the great thing in this world is not so much where we stand, as in what direction we are moving."

I used it with my players then and have used it in each of the past three years. When we win an important game, we don't sit around and try to figure out where we are at that time. We try to talk about in what direction are we moving. We try to say we're going to get better for the next game; we're going to prepare and be ready to play the next one.

I think all successful people, all true winners, have the ability to move beyond their previous accomplishments. Holmes' quote helps us look ahead, not look back at what has happened to us, whether it was positive or negative.

Here is a quote from Dr. Charles Garfield, a human behavioral scientist, that all Gators should heed: "A peak performer has the ability to transcend previous accomplishments, to not become complacent or overconfident, but to immediately start preparing for the next assignment."

I think the Gators' inability to transcend their previous accomplishments is something that has hampered us over the years. Often, too much attention has been paid to what is written and said in the media and by fans, and not enough given to the next task.

I believe one of the problems of annually playing Georgia the week after Auburn has been that when Florida has gone into the Georgia games as the favorite, after victories over the Tigers, they have been self-satisfied, complacent and not up to the difficult task at hand. Too many times over the years we have seen Florida teams record big victories over outstanding teams, but lose to inferior teams in games that our fans considered shocking upsets.

We want to emphasize the importance of transcending the past, because if you think and talk about your accomplishments too much it will hurt you in your next assignment. We have 11 games on our schedule, and each one of them is very important in its own right.

Sir Walter Raleigh once said, "There's a beginning to every mission, but a mission finished to the very end is what yields the true glory."

We used his quote at the Sugar Bowl following the 1991 season, but it didn't help – we lost to Notre Dame. Obviously, the mission of winning the first official conference championship, plus defeating FSU for the first time in five years, was all the true glory we could muster in 1991.

My approach to the games we play is that if your team is good enough to win by three or four touchdowns, then that's what you're supposed to do. Some people might say it's a little greedy to try to win by as many points as you can, but I believe that's the way the games are meant to be played.

I was taught that approach as a youngster growing up in Johnson City, Tennessee, by my coaches and my dad – the Reverend J. Graham Spurrier, who coached Little League and Babe Ruth League baseball.

One day before the Babe Ruth League season started my dad had our team – Thomas Products was the name – sitting out there in the grass along the right field line. He said, "Fellas, how many of you believe in the saying, 'It's not whether you win or lose, but how you play the game'?"

Well, about all the kids raised their hands because they had been taught that was a good saying, and they thought that's probably what this coach believes, so why not agree with him.

My dad then said he didn't believe in that saying. He said it does matter whether you win or lose – that's the reason they keep score. If it didn't matter, there wouldn't be any reason to keep score; there would be no need to have a winner and a loser. He told us that the game is meant to be played the best you can, and the first objective is to win, fairly and squarely within the rules.

I always have believed that totally. My philosophy on the way we approach a game is to try and score as many points as we can. If you're good enough to win by a big margin, that's what you should try to accomplish.

With that approach you eliminate a lot of close games. You

eliminate the situation in which you get ahead, become cautious and then have the other team hit a big play or two; all of a sudden you have a close game where who knows what's going to happen.

I don't care how good a team is; any team that plays a lot of close games is going to lose some of them. Basketball teams win by 25 to 30 points, baseball teams win games by 11 or 12 runs, and nobody gives it a second thought. Why should football be any different?

Nobody will ever accuse us of going into a "prevent" offense when we get ahead, you can count on that.

My theory on playing backup players is that you've got to let them play, not shackle them because you are way ahead. We let our backup players go out and play. Passing is a major part of our offense, so we're going to throw the ball no matter what the score is.

We will not call timeout to stop the clock or throw one into the end zone during the last 15 to 20 seconds of the game, but in the normal course of action I believe in letting your players play the game. If they score a touchdown, that's what they would like to do, and that's part of the fun of playing the game.

It's the other team's responsibility to stop them. I've been on the opposite side of it; and if the other team wants to score when they are way ahead of me, that's fine. Their players are having fun – that's football – and you've got to let your players play and coaches coach.

As coaches, we constantly strive to get our players to play the entire 60 minutes, and so we are going to coach for 60 minutes. If we quit, then they're going to think: Hey, you quit coaching the last two minutes of the game, and we thought we were supposed to play for 60 minutes.

I firmly believe this approach is a big part of the reason for our success here and at Duke, in that our team tried to win by three to four touchdowns; when we faltered a little, we won by only 10 to 12 points. At Duke we never knew what a safe lead was, so we assumed there was no such thing.

That's just my philosophy, and it's the philosophy we're going to keep and stress. We're going to coach our players to play as hard as they can every down and to try to win by a comfortable margin, if possible.

Every coach has his own thoughts about what it takes on the practice field to prepare his players and instill in them his fundamental approach to the game of football.

Some people have mentioned that at our practices the coaches aren't constantly screaming and criticizing players. This is something I thoroughly believe: As a coach, you coach first. Your overriding priority is to teach, teach, teach. There eventually comes a point, after you have exhausted your teaching and your encouraging, where if a player is not giving the effort, not paying attention, loafing, then it is time to criticize.

A player has to do a lot for our coaches to yell at him or criticize him, but we'll certainly do it if it reaches a point when he doesn't respond to our coaching, teaching and encouraging. Our job is to make sure each player is progressing toward becoming the best he can, given his basic talent.

We try to eliminate as much contact as possible during practice. Football is a rough sport, dangerous at times. Injuries can happen almost any day at practice and certainly in any game. The more contact you have, the more injuries you are going to have.

Our players have heard me say many, many times, "We don't play ourselves. Florida is not on our schedule. Our practices are for the purpose of getting ready for our opponents."

What we try to do in practice is learn to beat our SEC and out-of-conference opponents. We do have to hit each other; we have to practice hitting so we will be ready to hit with proper fundamental techniques and at full speed when the games come.

However, we definitely separate practices from games, and we tell our players not to hit a teammate if he is in a position where he is vulnerable to injury. Occasionally, a player will accidentally hit a guy low or in a way that could lead to injury, and the first thing I do is tell him he is wrong. You've got to lay off that hit if it could lead to hurting a teammate.

I know so many coaching staffs that make scrimmages so

competitive that coaches are yelling and screaming at each other, players are fighting, and who wins that day takes on almost life-or-death importance.

In all of our scrimmages, we do not keep score. We tell our players: We want you to improve as individuals. If you'll improve and play your position and techniques with maximum effort, then you are going to help the team.

And we try our best as coaches to eliminate making our scrimmages overly competitive battles between the offense and defense. We don't want our players thinking us vs. them, offense vs. defense. I believe this helps the players understand that we are in this thing together, that the reason we practice is to make us a better team.

I think we have an obligation to parents not to expose their sons to any unnecessary risk of injury. In that regard, I believe that players who have started for you and have proven they can play the game will be ready to play; they don't need to scrimmage a lot. They don't need to play in all the practice games and the spring games.

To me, spring games are for the younger players who haven't played much under pressure in front of a crowd. It's a chance for these players to gain experience playing in a stadium in front of a fairly large crowd.

During the spring game of 1991, I did not play any of the seniors, I guess for the first time in Florida football history. This caused a little commotion in the athletic department. Some thought that since we were charging two dollars, some fans might not think they were getting their money's worth.

I told the administration that I've got to do what I believe is best for Florida football, and it would be stupid of us to send Brad Culpepper, Tony McCoy or any of the other outstanding seniors out there in the Orange and Blue Game where they could get a knee blown out.

This game is nothing but preparation for our real games against conference opponents and the other teams on our schedule. I think everybody has pretty much accepted that this is how we're going to run future Orange and Blue contests.

We believe the University of Florida has the resources and opportunity to win championships as often as anybody. Preparing the team to accomplish that is our mission as coaches.

You've got to run your program the best way you know, go play the games and see what happens.

2

FLORIDA:
A COACH'S DREAM

ometime in life you have to find out what kind of person you are, to see if you're good enough and smart enough to coach against the best in your profession.

Coaching at Florida presents the challenge of coaching against the finest teams and coaches in the country. Although coming back to my alma mater was certainly something special, this challenge was the biggest reason I wanted the Gator coaching position.

It really wasn't a hard decision once I was offered the job, but I needed to hear out other teams, like the Atlanta Falcons and the Phoenix Cardinals of the NFL, to be certain about my decision.

When I told Tom Butters, Duke's athletic director, that I was taking the Florida job, the major reason I cited was the challenge of coaching Florida to the heights that many people believed the university could and should be reaching.

If I wanted only security and excellent treatment for me and my family, I would have stayed at Duke. It was a great situation. We enjoyed the community and the people we worked with.

There are certainly many advantages to coaching in that environment. But if you're a competitor, you wonder what it would be like to have the chance to coach the best athletes in the country against other similarly talented athletes.

I've been asked many times by many people if being the head coach at Florida was always my ultimate goal in coaching. I have to say that it wasn't, because I didn't know whether the job there would ever be open during my career.

It seems that most coaches who are successful are able to coach for about 20 to 25 years. If the head coaching position at Florida had been stable, there might never have been an opportunity for me to coach there.

My goal was to be a Division I head coach. I felt that if I just applied myself I had the talent to be a head coach, considering that there are more than 100 of these jobs out there.

Having the opportunity to coach at the University of Florida is a coach's dream, something just about every coach in America would love to have come true. The Gators have all the advantages in college football. First of all, our school is a highly regarded academic university – a member of the prestigious American Association of Universities along with other state universities such as Texas, North Carolina and Virginia, and such private schools as Vanderbilt, Duke and Rice.

We have the best support of any school in the SEC. The fans contribute more money here than at any other school in the conference. Our stadium is the largest in the state – college or professional – with about 85,000 seats. The crowds for our six home games in 1991 were the six largest football crowds in state history.

Football in the state is probably the best in the nation. In 1991, the recruiting classes of Florida, Miami and FSU all were ranked among the top five in the nation. This helps demonstrate how super the high school coaching and talent are in this state.

What we at Florida need to do is do a good job of recruiting in our home state, do things the right way and be successful on the field. We have to make certain our players are graduating, and, according to the 1991 College Football Association survey, our graduation rate was 81 percent. That put us among a prestigious group of colleges such as Duke, Stanford, Northwestern, Rice, Michigan and Virginia.

So how did I get this great coaching job?

During the 1989 season, at about 8:30 on Sunday morning, October 8, a friend of mine on the athletic board at the University of Florida called and told me that Galen Hall was resigning as the Gators' head coach later that day.

"You need to keep it quiet," he said, "but the head coaching job is going to be available. They're going to announce an interim coach, but at the end of the season the job will be open."

At first I was a little bit stunned. I like Galen. We got to know each other over the years – we played some golf together – and he is a wonderful person. I didn't know all the reasons behind what was happening at Florida, and at the time I really was more concerned about my Duke team.

That team was in the process of winning six straight conference games, and winning the ACC championship had my full attention. In the back of my mind I realized that there was a good chance I eventually would be offered the head coaching job at Florida because of the success I'd had with the Tampa Bay Bandits and at Duke.

The week after Duke beat North Carolina in the final game of the '89 season, I got a visit in Durham from Dr. Robert Bryan, the interim president at Florida; Bill Arnsparger, the athletic director; and Dr. Nick Cassisi, a member of the athletic board who now is faculty athletic representative.

They came out to my house for our first visit. We talked briefly, and it seemed Dr. Bryan wanted to go ahead and offer me the job then. He had Arnsparger talk about the salary and what the job entailed.

I told them we didn't need to get into any details because I had already told the Duke team that I was going to coach them through the All-American Bowl game against Texas Tech in Birmingham. It was a commitment I was going to honor. After that game, I would consider what looked best for me and my family, then make a decision. I just didn't think it was right to make any agreements before Thanksgiving, and Dr. Bryan agreed.

I did ask them how the university could do a better job of graduating its players, because I had seen graduation percentages that had bothered me. Certainly you can play football and graduate from the University of Florida, and I felt graduation should always be a top priority.

Dr. Bryan was very instrumental in my hiring. In my opinion, he is a great Gator. He made me feel comfortable with the Florida situation and very welcome.

Coach Arnsparger did come back up to Durham one more time. We had dinner together and talked a little bit about what was involved with the job, the weekly radio and television shows, and the contract. He also made me feel comfortable about being wanted as the head coach, and we worked extremely well together during his remaining tenure as athletic director.

In mid-December I had a chance to get away for a couple of days, so we set up a meeting in Gainesville at Dr. Bryan's house – the UF president's official residence.

I spent the night before the meeting at the home of players' rep Bill O'Neal, on a lake near Melrose. "Uncle Willie" has been a good friend to our family and a good friend to Florida football players since the 1960s. When I was a player at Florida we used to go out – back then it was legal – and eat dinner with Bill and his wonderful wife, Katie.

He has been the agent for many players and was mine when I was drafted by the San Francisco 49ers in 1967. He has helped me through all the years, and so, naturally, I asked him to represent me in contract negotiations with Florida officials.

I showed "Uncle Willie" a list of what I wanted that night and told him that if the University of Florida would meet all the requests on that list, I was ready to become the head coach of the Gators.

Bill studied the list. At first he said he didn't know if Florida would meet all my requests. He told me I needed to understand that their job was to hire me as cheaply as they could, and our job was to get paid as well as we could, and that there would be some tough negotiations going on.

I told him I didn't think it would be that way. Two NFL teams were talking with me, and my requests were in line with what I believed the university could pay its head football coach. I really thought they would hire me at what was fair and in line with what some other college head coaches were making.

Around 5 p.m. the next day we met with Dr. Bryan. He had the university attorney, Tom MacDonald, with him, along with Arnsparger, Cassisi and senior associate athletic director Jeremy Foley. So, basically, the people who were responsible for hiring the new football coach were all gathered in one spot.

I spelled out my requests to this group. Dr. Bryan went down the list point by point, asking MacDonald, "Can we do that?" "Can we do that?" all down the line. The answer was "yes" each time.

It was probably the easiest contract "Uncle Willie" had ever negotiated – no arguing, no hassling. Dr. Bryan set the tone at that meeting, and about the only item we debated was when to make the announcement.

We wound up putting all the details in place, but we didn't strike the final agreement that day. We decided to make the contract final after the bowl games involving Duke and Florida, and we agreed that no more negotiating was needed.

At that time, we felt this was the best way to proceed. In our opinion it was best to allow Duke's coaches to coach the Devils against Texas Tech and Florida's coaches to coach the Gators against Washington in the Freedom Bowl.

After our bowl game I drove over to our family condominium at Crescent Beach and called Coach Arnsparger to inform him that I was accepting their offer to become the head coach at Florida. He immediately called a press conference for December 31, 1989, to make the announcement.

3

A PASSING STYLE

Our passing game originated at Duke University in 1980 when Coach Red Wilson hired me as offensive coordinator. He told me he was looking for someone who could bring in a passing offense, and that I would have free rein.

Having total authority to install an offense was tremendous freedom for an assistant coach. When I asked him if he wanted to retain Duke's previous terminology and numbering system, he said to call it whatever I wanted – the offense was all mine.

I was able to experiment, even in games, to see how something would work.

COACH RED WILSON:

I quickly realized Steve has a great, great imagination. He sees things very few people see. And I don't know how he sees it.

I've always felt that most offenses I've been involved with are either complicated or don't give the players the best opportunity to be successful. I try to give our players a chance to do only what they are physically able to do. In other words, if an offensive lineman can't knock a defensive lineman backward, why should you ask him to do it? But if he can get in front of him and push and shove and pass block, as well as play as hard as he can, then we certainly are going to have a chance to throw the ball and be successful.

I'm not going to ask a quarterback to attempt a throw he's not capable of making. And, likewise, I'm not going to ask a wide receiver to run routes he can't run.

Through trial and error we developed a lot of good plays. Basically, there is a good pass play for every defense. There isn't any one great defense that can shut down the pass or everybody would be using it.

It's exciting when you develop a pass play and it works. Sometimes I'll wake up at four or five o'clock in the morning with an idea, and I can't wait to get out to the field and try it.

What we try to do – and this was developed at Duke from 1980 to 1982 and then with the Bandits – is have a good play called for every defense. We try to have a good pass pattern called with good protection; and if we execute it, we have a good chance of being successful.

I've been around so many coaches who, when a play failed, said, "We just didn't have a good play on." If this happens very many times during a game, you don't have a very good chance of being successful.

Though you always try to have a good play on, sometimes you don't. But if we can minimize the number of bad plays, we can be successful throwing the ball against any defense.

We're constantly refining the offense, looking for new formations. The routes are very similar. If a team has a deep zone coverage, then we have to throw in front of them. If they're playing tight and challenging us, then we must be able to throw it over their heads. If they're playing tight underneath man coverage with some guys behind them helping out, then we need to throw more to our backs one-on-one against linebackers.

What we try to do is see the defense and call the play that has the best chance to be successful against it if we protect, throw and catch properly.

Ben Bennett was the first quarterback to perform in this system. He was there in 1980 and wound up breaking a lot of NCAA passing records during his career.

I remember in the first game of the 1980 season, I'd call a pass play and the defense would be in the wrong coverage for it. Next time I'd call a play hoping they would be in another coverage. Our opponent, East Carolina, used a couple of coverages: a two-deep zone and a three-deep zone.

There were some good patterns to use against each defense, so after the game I asked the wide receivers if they could see the difference between those two coverages. They said they could. I asked Bennett, the quarterback, if he could see whether they were in the two-deep or three-deep zone, and he said he could.

That's when I decided we would start running some pass-option plays; we were going to give a wide receiver a chance to either run this route or that route according to what he saw in the defense. The quarterback then would make his choice based on what he saw the defense doing.

From trial and error, experimenting in practice and games and making up plays, we developed this offense. It has no limits as to how it grows. We're still trying to develop new plays. I've had them come to me while jogging or on the road; I've drawn up some good ones on napkins at breakfast.

I read somewhere that to be successful you either do things better than everybody else, or you have to do things differently than everybody else. At Duke, our best chance to be successful was to do things differently.

I knew at Duke University we were not going to win games if I tried to outcoach everybody else while using the same offense all the other teams used. Our personnel was not better than our opponents', and in many instances it was not as good.

We had to come up with different plays that would give our players a chance to be successful. I think every coach in America would benefit from coaching at a school that's the underdog most of the time. If you can learn to win games when you're the underdog, certainly you will have a chance to win a lot of games when you're the favorite.

BEN BENNETT, DUKE QUARTERBACK (1980-83):

What Coach Spurrier did at Duke was absolutely phenomenal, going 7-3-1 and 8-4 and winning the ACC with the type of personnel he had. What he did with the offense when I was there is a tremendous credit to his genius.

At Florida we obviously have better personnel than we had at Duke. Still, we are refining and trying to improve the offensive system in order to help the players be successful. We want our quarterbacks to know where they are going to throw the ball without making it too complicated.

Over the years people have insisted that our quarterbacks are all products of the offensive system, but that is far from correct. It takes the right kind of quarterback to operate the system properly because he is so involved in the on-field choices in reacting to the various defensive alignments.

Shane Matthews certainly didn't vault from fifth team in the spring to starter in the fall – with four more experienced quarterbacks ahead of him – because of the system. He proved he could make the system successful. The qualities Shane Matthews has are what you look for in a quarterback.

What we ask of the quarterback, after he looks over the defense at the line of scrimmage, is to decide whether the play called is the right one against that defense. If it is OK, he should leave it on. If it's not very good, we ask him to get us to the best play possible against the defense he sees.

Once we've got that play called, he drops back to throw and we generally send five receivers out. We don't tell him to throw to this one, this one or that one. We tell him to throw to the best receiver possible on the play.

We tell him to look at the defense and then make a choice, a decision on which one would be the best to throw to in that particular situation. If possible, we would like to throw deep first. If a guy's open deep, that's where we want to throw it. We are always pushing to go downfield with the ball.

If the deep receivers aren't open, we next want to attempt to throw it to a receiver open in the intermediate area, somewhere between 12 and 18 yards from the line of scrimmage. If those receivers are covered, we come back to our short receiver guy, the guy who's slipped out of the backfield or a tight end coming underneath the coverage about four or five yards down field.

Not only does the quarterback have to make a choice on where to throw it, he makes a choice on when to throw it. Sometimes he goes back and sets up, pauses a little bit and then dumps the ball off to a back or tight end. This, along with draw plays, tends to slow down a constant hard rush by the defense.

So the quarterbacks in our system have all been special people to me because of the way they have worked and adapted to the mental aspect as well as the physical. We've had success for many reasons, but such quarterbacks as Ben Bennett, Steve Slayden, Anthony Dilweg, Billy Ray, David Brown and Shane Matthews have been the key figures.

The quarterback must be intelligent and poised under pressure. That is more important than pure physical ability. You try to have a plan before you go back, but you have to keep thinking as you prepare to take the snap and then as you get the ball.

The quarterback needs to know and understand the whole picture, where the receivers are going, the different coverages and fronts. He must know what to do and when to do it.

Our evaluations of a quarterback prospect aren't always the same as those of other coaches who are looking at the same player. We have turned down some quarterback prospects who the recruiting services ranked among the best in the nation. They might become fine players at other schools, but I'm confident we have a good understanding of what it will take for a player at this vital position to be successful in our offense.

We try to give a lot of freedom to the quarterback and with

that comes the responsibility for him to make good choices and not make the crucial mistakes that beat you.

We're all proud of what our quarterbacks have accomplished over the years: Bennett completed his career as the NCAA's all-time leading passer with 9,614 yards from 1980-83; Slayden led the ACC in total offense in 1987; Dilweg was the ACC Player of the Year in 1988 and set conference records for total offense, passing and TD passes; and the combination of Ray and Brown finished fourth in the nation and led the ACC in passing in 1989.

Shane's career at Florida has been brilliant and record-shattering; he has been named Southeastern Conference Player of the Year for two straight seasons.

We don't throw the ball at the expense of the running game. Our 1991 SEC championship team had 397 rushing attempts as compared to 390 passing attempts. We had a 1,000-yard rusher at Duke in Randy Cuthbert and one at Florida in Errict Rhett, who led the conference in rushing in '91.

In the big picture, we strive to have a balanced offense, but we don't go out each week and say we need to run it 50 percent of the time and pass it 50 percent. Depending on the defense we are facing, it could be heavily slanted toward either running or passing in any particular game.

However, instead of the running game setting up the passing game, which is normal in many offenses, our passing game sets up the running game. We are going to feature the draw off the passing game as our top rushing play. And we're basically going to get the ball up the field, be an attacking offense for the entire game – no matter the score. If we're way ahead we still will put it in the air because that's our game.

Although we won't call a timeout to stop the clock to get one more score, we might be throwing it down field on the last play of the game.

RON ZOOK, FLORIDA DEFENSIVE COORDINATOR:

I'm glad we don't have to play against this offense with Coach Spurrier directing it. What it does is utilize all five eligi-

ble receivers – sometimes six of them when you count the quarterback. It forces you to cover the entire field and all eligible receivers, putting an enormous stretch on the defense.

As soon as you try to drop back and cover all receivers, they gash you with the run. It's an offense that always has new wrinkles and tends to slow down the defense because you are looking for what's going to happen next.

This offense will go from two backs to no backs from down to down. There is no way a defense has time to prepare for all the things you will face.

It's difficult to blitz the quarterback because he doesn't hold the football. He throws it on time and throws it where you aren't. That is a major key to the offense.

Now there are many people going to the passing game. I believe we have an advantage in its use because of Coach Spurrier's knowledge of what he is trying to accomplish. He is very unpredictable and sees things under the pressure of a game situation that very, very few coaches can see.

He's amazing and uncanny, and defenses have to be careful about getting into a guessing game with him, because he will figure out what they are doing and burn them.

4

FIVE CRUCIAL GAMES

Five crucial games in my coaching career have been turning points in the direction my career has taken:

- Georgia Tech vs. Duke, 1979
- Duke vs. Virginia, 1981
- Duke vs. Tennessee, 1982
- Tampa Bay Bandits vs. Philadelphia Stars, 1983
- Duke vs. Clemson, 1989

GEORGIA TECH VS. DUKE, 1979

In 1979 I was coaching for Pepper Rodgers at Georgia Tech. I'd started my career in 1978 under Doug Dickey at Florida, but when Coach Dickey was fired after that season, only a couple of assistants were kept. Luckily, I had the chance to go to Tech the next season.

As quarterback coach I called a few plays here and there, mostly pass plays; our offensive coordinator, Larry Travis, called a lot of the plays, as did Pepper.

We really struggled that season. We were 1-5-1, owning a big victory over William and Mary and a tie with Florida, which lost the other 10 games on its schedule. We had gone back to the Wishbone offense against Tulane, losing a close game in New Orleans 12-7.

The following Monday while on my regular noontime jog, I decided to go ask Coach Rodgers if he would let me call the plays and act as the offensive coordinator that week in the game against Duke.

I finally got up enough nerve to talk to him. I told him that I appreciated his hiring me and providing an opportunity, since without this job I would be back home in Gainesville looking for work. Then I told him I would really like to help him, help Georgia Tech and help the football team, and that I was very confident I could do a good job of putting in the plays during the week and calling them in the game.

I mentioned that Coach Dickey had gained enough confidence in me to allow me to do that in several games in 1978, and that I would like to have that authority for the game against Duke.

"Spurrier, you got it," Pepper said. "I'll tell the other coaches that it's your show this week, that you'll come down to the sidelines and call the plays. Go ahead. It's all yours."

Man, I was so excited. I went down and started drawing up ball plays and getting the offensive game plan ready, and we worked on it all week.

Early in the game we threw five consecutive passes, and Coach Travis, our offensive line coach as well as the offensive coordinator, looked at me and said, "Are we ever going to run the ball?"

"Maybe," I replied. "But not now."

We had a good game offensively and beat Duke 24-14, which started a three-game winning streak during which Coach Rodgers allowed me to call the plays and act as the offensive coordinator.

That game was a crucial first test of my ability to call plays at Georgia Tech but, more importantly, the game was against Duke.

Their coach, Red Wilson, and athletic director, Tom Butters, really liked what we did offensively that day.

Coach Rodgers was fired after the 1979 season, and it turns out Duke was looking for a coach who could come in, put in a passing game and play wide-open football. So, looking back, the opportunity to act as the offensive coach in that Georgia Tech-Duke game gave me the chance to become the offensive coordinator at Duke the following year.

The timing certainly had been right.

DUKE VS. VIRGINIA, 1981

My first year at Duke in 1980 we were only 2-9, upsetting Clemson on a day when everything went right for us but losing a bunch of close games. Starting the next season, Coach Wilson was under a lot of pressure to win some games and be competitive. It was a tense situation.

We opened up on the road against Ohio State and South Carolina and didn't do very well against these two quality opponents, losing to both of them. The third game of the season we went to Virginia, which was in a similar situation at 0-2 with Coach Dick Bestwick also under pressure to do better.

Tom Butters, our athletic director, did not attend the game. The word was he was out watching another game somewhere else, looking for a new head coach. I was in my third coaching job in four years and certainly didn't want to be out hunting another position so soon.

Ben Bennett, our starting quarterback, was out of the game; he had sprained his shoulder against Ohio State. Ron Sally, a reserve quarterback, came on and began a five-game stretch in which he played tremendously well for us.

The Virginia game rocked back and forth, and at the start of the fourth quarter we were behind 24-15. I was up top in the press box calling the plays and telling Eddie Williamson, our offensive line coach, to keep the players excited because we still had a chance.

He told me there were a lot of long faces down on the sidelines, and not much in the way of confidence. That was to be expected, because Duke University had not come from behind to win a game in a final quarter since anyone could remember.

But some good things started happening for us. Cedric Jones, an all-conference wide receiver who later played about 10 years for the New England Patriots, caught a deep pass, and we had a first down on about the three-yard line. We managed to run it in from there to make the score 24-22.

We got the ball back, and on second-and-one at midfield, we lined up in a two-tight-end formation and faked a run. While they were trying to stuff the line of scrimmage, we threw the ball over the free safety's head to Jones, who took it down to the six-yard line. We ran it in to put us ahead 29-24, held on for the minute that was left and got one of the most important victories of my career.

What that game did was give our team confidence that we could beat quality opponents, and it took some pressure off Coach Wilson. We went on to win six of our last nine games to finish with a 6-5 record, Duke's first winning record in seven years.

DUKE VS. TENNESSEE, 1982

In 1982 we opened the season with a victory over an outstanding Tennessee team in Knoxville. Tennessee had excellent players like Reggie White, who has been all-pro with the Philadelphia Eagles for several years, and Willie Gault, the Olympic sprinter and NFL star.

It was a game in which Tennessee punted only a couple of times, but we didn't punt much either. Our fullback, Greg Boone, ran a kickoff back 104 yards for a touchdown, and Ben Bennett hit Chris Castor on an 88-yard touchdown pass.

We also ran the ball. In the fourth quarter a back-up tailback, Joel Blunk, rushed for more than 100 yards.

The thing I remember best about this game is that we had the ball on our one-yard line with a 25-24 lead and 9:30 remaining in the game, and somehow we managed to move it the length of the field to Tennessee's one-yard line, consuming all the time on the clock. We ran a quarterback sneak on the last play of the game to kill the clock.

That was an emotional victory over a good Tennessee team. It gave credibility to Duke football and to the style of offense we were using.

In the last game of that season we beat a good North Carolina team for our first victory over the Tar Heels in 10 years, holding the ball for more than 40 minutes, making 32 first downs and generating 500 yards of offense.

Carl Franks, who coaches with me at Florida now, caught the winning touchdown pass in a 23-17 game. The Duke students tore down the goal posts there at Wallace Wade Stadium and passed them up through the stands. It seemed like the students stayed there forever, very reminiscent of Florida's game against Florida State in 1991, when the fans simply didn't want to leave the stadium.

We had opened that 1982 season with three consecutive wins, over Tennessee, South Carolina and Virginia, and it was at this time that the United States Football League was being organized. John Bassett, the owner of the Tampa Bay Bandits, was in the process of hiring a coach.

We'd had the great victory over Tennessee and were leading the ACC in passing and total offense when Bassett flew up from Tampa to see me the night before our game against Virginia Tech.

Bugsy Engelberg, the Bandits' general manager, had told me Mr. Bassett just wanted to come and have dinner with me, and that he wasn't going to hire a coach anytime soon. I told Red Wilson that the owner of the Bandits wanted to take me to dinner Friday night, and he said that was OK with him.

Mr. Bassett was accompanied by Bandit limited partners Don Dizney and Maston O'Neal. Waiting until the drive back to the airport, Mr. Bassett said he wanted me to become the head coach of the Bandits. He told me to get with Bugsy, who would draw up a contract.

I told Mr. Bassett I appreciated the offer and would take the job, but I couldn't leave Duke until the season was over. He said that was fine; later Mr. O'Neal told me that Mr. Bassett had been impressed that I would not leave my team at Duke in the lurch.

That's how I got hired by the Bandits at age 37 – the youngest of the nation's 40 professional head coaches.

The NFL experts told Mr. Bassett that he was crazy for hiring an assistant college coach. They said I would be eaten alive in the USFL by former NFL head coaches such as Chuck Fairbanks, Red Miller and George Allen, and by the NFL assistants who were being hired as USFL head coaches.

Mr. Bassett didn't care too much about public opinion. If he had his facts in place and felt good about a person, he would go ahead and give him an opportunity.

Certainly I owe a great deal of credit for my coaching career to John Bassett, who took a gamble on a young offensive coordinator from Duke University and made him head coach of a professional team.

As it turned out, there were only three coaches who lasted all three years in the league – me, Jim Mora of the Philadelphia (and then Baltimore) Stars and Rollie Dotsch of the Birmingham Stallions.

TAMPA BAY BANDITS VS. PHILADELPHIA STARS, 1983

The Bandits opened that first season of 1983 in Tampa Stadium against the Boston Breakers, selling more than 42,000 tickets.

We got the kickoff and came out in the no-huddle offense. At that time I don't think many fans, if any, had ever seen the no-huddle offense. Of course, everyone is using it now. Most people think it started with the Cincinnati Bengals, but I believe the Bandits were one of the first teams to use it.

I've used the no-huddle in just about every game since then, and we try to use it a lot at Florida.

The USFL fans really appreciated the way we would gamble, not always playing everything by the book. It was exciting, entertaining football because we were always willing to take calculated risks.

The fourth crucial game of my coaching career was the fourth game of the Bandits' inaugural season of 1983. We were 3-0 and our opponents, the Philadelphia Stars, were 3-0, so you had the league's two unbeaten teams playing at Veterans Stadium in Philadelphia.

It was a challenging coaching matchup. A bunch of college coaches would face a group of NFL coaches for the first time, outside of the old College All-Star Game held annually in Chicago until 1974.

My staff of former college coaches included defensive coordinator Charlie Bailey, defensive line coach Barry Wilson and Jack Burns, who is now offensive coordinator of the Minnesota Vikings. He was my wide receiver coach that first year and then switched to running backs coach.

Playing against all those NFL coaches in Philadelphia, we won the game by getting a big early lead and holding on. It was a game that won us respect all around the league.

Other owners started calling Mr. Bassett and asking him how in the world he was doing it at Tampa Bay. The Bandits had the cheapest payroll in the league and the lowest-paid coaches, and still they were beating all the other teams. Mr. Bassett told them it was just smart selection of players and coaches and his organization. Mr. Bassett was really tickled to receive all those calls.

We were on top of the world there for a while. When the USFL folded after the 1985 season I was still under contract to the Bandits. I didn't coach in 1986, but did interview with two or three schools that year.

The Tampa Bay Buccaneers job was open then. Since I lived there in Tampa and had a proven record, I was hoping to get the position, but it wasn't to be. The owner selected Ray Perkins of

Alabama, starting a chain reaction that eventually led to my getting the head coaching job at Duke. When Perkins left Alabama, Steve Sloan – head coach at Duke University – left Duke to become athletic director for the Crimson Tide. This created an opening for head coach at the school where I had been an assistant coach for three wonderful years.

Tom Butters, Duke's athletic director and a good friend, hired me in January 1987. It was a fortunate turn of events. My family loved the area and I had thoroughly enjoyed the school and the people working there – and, of course, I was unemployed at the time.

DUKE VS. CLEMSON, 1989

By 1988 we had it going pretty well, finishing with a 7-3-1 record that year, the best record in 26 years for Duke University. Going into the 1989 season we felt we had a chance to have a fine year.

Our goals were high, but we opened up losing three of our first four games to good teams. We lost at Tennessee, at South Carolina and at Virginia. Our lone victory was at home against Northwestern.

The fifth game of the season would be at home at Wallace Wade Stadium against Clemson, the seventh-ranked team in the nation.

We were 0-1 in the ACC after losing to Virginia 49-28. Virginia had eight possessions in the game, scoring seven touchdowns and missing a field goal on an attempt that hit the uprights. We didn't even slow them down and never forced a punt.

After that game I really was frustrated and upset with the way we were playing and coaching, and said that our chances of beating Clemson were "a million to one." This got into the newspapers the next week. Clemson head coach Danny Ford responded that if Duke feels that way about the game, he didn't see why we should even play it.

I got with our defensive coaches – Bob Sanders and Jim Collins – that week, and told them we were going to blitz, blitz, blitz from then on. We were struggling on defense, not making anything good happen.

My theory was that if they throw a touchdown pass or make a long run on a blitz, that's fine; but we're going to put some pressure on the other team, and at least force them to punt the football at times. We had an excellent offense, and we needed to get the ball more often to be able to outscore the opponent.

We were just not good enough to play sound basic defense. We started this blitz philosophy the week of the Clemson game, playing almost the entire afternoon with nine players at the line of scrimmage.

We had an emotional meeting the night before the game. We had seen a war movie, *In Country*, that put goosebumps on many of us. It was a story about a girl whose father had been killed in the Vietnam War, and it starred Bruce Willis.

With the players' emotions running high from watching the movie, I felt I didn't need to say much in the meeting to pump them up. So I simply asked all the players to shake hands with me and with the other coaches right before they went to bed Friday night. We didn't talk about any "X's and O's." We just said we're going to go out and play and coach as hard as we can on every play, and not be concerned about the score at any time during the game.

The next day I could sense that the players had slept on this and had made a commitment.

There was a steady drizzle on game day. Though Clemson was a much faster team, the wet field neutralized their tremendous speed and brought them down to our level.

It was a funny game: We moved the ball consistently in the first half, but something bad would always happen. We had Keith Ewell, our fastest wide receiver, open behind their secondary by 10 yards, but a perfect pass hit him on the face mask and bounced away.

We were behind 14-0 at halftime, but in the locker room our players were still excited. They felt they could play with Clemson; that the Tigers were not running it down our throats and that our offense was moving the ball. Everybody just wanted to go out and keep playing hard; we felt that eventually something good would happen.

In the third quarter on third-and-30 our quarterback threw the ball as far as he could. Clemson's Dexter Davis intercepted the pass but then fumbled as he was trying to cut. We recovered on Clemson's 23-yard line, and it was almost like a gift from heaven.

On second down at their four-yard line Randy Cuthbert ran off tackle behind Chris Port and Bud Zuberer. It looked like a rugby scrum – a huge pile of people pushing and shoving, and Cuthbert's legs churning away as the entire pile moved all the way into the end zone; it was our first touchdown of the day.

This gave us momentum, and we ran the ball at them for eight to 10 yards at a pop. Billy Ray threw a touchdown pass from the 19 to Clarkston Hines, and suddenly it was a 14-14 tie.

They kicked a field goal early in the fourth quarter to take a 17-14 lead. We got the ball back on our 25 with time for one last drive. We got down to their eight-yard line, and I noticed on second down they had failed to cover our fullback coming out of the backfield. I immediately signaled in the Bopper Play – in which the fullback is our primary receiver – and Chris Brown was wide open for a touchdown. We held on to win 21-17.

It was such a big game for all of us; we believed that if we could beat Clemson we could beat any team in the ACC. We went on to win six straight conference games, finishing as co-champions with Virginia at 6-1.

By winning against Clemson, Duke gained the confidence and momentum to win the ACC, capturing eight victories in a season for the first time in 29 years. This success put me in position to earn the job at the University of Florida, and got the interest of a lot of pro teams as well. The Atlanta Falcons and Phoenix Cardinals came to Durham to talk to me about their head coaching positions.

After we beat North Carolina 41-0 in the last game of the '89 season, I told our players that I was going to be their coach through the bowl game on December 28, but that I couldn't guarantee that I'd be with them after that.

The opportunity and challenge to coach at the University of Florida was something I could not turn down. I believe the players and fans of Duke have come to understand that my decision to accept the Florida job was one that I had to make.

5

LEARNING TO WIN

Vince Lombardi, the legendary coach of the Green Bay Packers, said it best: "Winning is a habit. Unfortunately, so is losing."

Returning to Florida as head coach in 1990, I saw it was obvious that we needed to change the habit of losing crucial games. Gator teams, including mine when I was a player in the 1960s, just couldn't seem to play well when the championship was on the line.

The joke "Wait 'til next year" had been dangling around the necks of Gators almost since Florida became a charter member of the Southeastern Conference in 1933.

Bad habits die hard. At Florida, we desperately needed to develop the attitude of a champion – the attitude that we're good enough to win and that if we go out and play as hard as we can, we can expect to be successful. However, until you win those big games, there still are doubts in everyone's mind.

That first team I inherited at Florida had a lot of talent, but they had not won the crucial game, the game that would put them in position to win a championship.

That team was 0-9 against Auburn, Georgia and FSU during the previous three years. Many of the players had been around for all nine of those losses.

We would have an early opportunity in 1990 to see if the motivational talks with the team during spring practice and in the preseason had been helpful in developing the attitude of a winner. Our second game of the season would be against defending conference champion Alabama in Tuscaloosa.

The opening game of my Florida head coaching career had been most encouraging, a 50-7 rout of outmanned Oklahoma State and a wonderful start for our rookie quarterback, Shane Matthews.

That game was at Florida Field in front of 75,428 excited Gator fans. The team was ready to play. You could hear a pin drop at our team meal the night before the game, and you could tell all the players were concentrating on the task at hand.

The win encouraged me, but our first big test was to come in Tuscaloosa the next week. For us to have a chance to win the conference championship we had to defeat Alabama or Tennessee on the road.

Until Friday night in Birmingham everything appeared normal. We had a good week of practice, flew into Tuscaloosa, had a nice workout, and then took the bus to the Wynfrey Hotel in Birmingham, where we spent the night.

Our routine on Friday night of game week is to have a team meal at 7 p.m., allow the players to watch a movie in their rooms, then meet for a snack at 9:30, followed by offensive and defensive meetings. Curfew is 11 p.m.

At the team meal on this first road trip, I discovered our players didn't know how to get ready to win a big game. Their behavior just amazed me. What a difference between the night before our opening game in Gainesville and this night in Birmingham. The guys laughed and giggled and carried on.

The week before, you could tell that mentally they were really getting ready to play. On the road, our players acted like they were on vacation. They were bubbly, and that is not a good sign.

They didn't seem to understand that they were getting ready to play the most important game of their careers. It became obvious to me that the way they acted must have contributed heavily to their lack of success in the past.

In my brief experience as a head coach, I have found that it's best if players are not deadly quiet, but in a restrained mood in which they are thinking about the next day's game.

As they were starting to eat, after one of the players had given the blessing, their conversation and laughter just kept getting louder. I took about all of it that I could stand, then I stood up and rapped my knife against a glass to get their attention.

I said, "Fellas, we're going to get our tails kicked tomorrow if you continue to laugh and giggle and not understand how important this game is. I guarantee you, Alabama's not laughing and giggling at their pregame meal. They're concentrating and getting mentally prepared to kick our tails good, and that's exactly what is going to happen if we don't start thinking about this game coming up."

The guys got quiet; they could tell I was very upset. I seemed afraid that we were going to get clobbered the next day, when actually we had a team with a good chance to beat Alabama on the road.

Maybe my speech got their attention a little bit. The mood certainly changed as the players became much, much quieter, and we had a good meeting later that night. It looked like they were starting to concentrate on the game, on a good chance to beat a quality SEC team.

ASSISTANT HEAD COACH JERRY ANDERSON:

The coaches were concerned because this was the complete opposite of the week before. It was our first road game, and they appeared distracted; and having been on the staff previously, I had seen this happen before. Coach Spurrier's remarks were straight to the point and easy to understand. The assistant coaches thought he set the tone for us to get focused on what we needed to do to beat Alabama.

We kicked off before noon, Central time, because the game was being telecast nationally on superstation WTBS. On the way over, I thought about what a great opportunity this was to knock down the mental barriers that surrounded Florida football.

The year before, the Gators had not won a game on TV, and they really hadn't beaten any good teams in recent years. This team needed to start learning how to win and not make excuses, and there would be no better time or place than that day at Bryant-Denny Stadium.

Walking out on that field where Coach Paul (Bear) Bryant had walked during his legendary career was an exciting experience. Many coaches have tried to emulate him, but there was only one Coach Bryant. I thought back to when he had tried to recruit me out of high school in Johnson City, Tennessee, and about the respect I had for him then and still do today.

The game got going and we struggled. We really struggled the entire first half, and it wasn't a very good show for the 8,000 Gator fans who had come up to Alabama, or for those watching on television.

I didn't feel I called a very good offensive game in that half. We'd put in a new play for tight end Kirk Kirkpatrick, an option route where he either hooks up or breaks outside depending on the coverage.

They had two guys covering Kirk the entire game. Bill Oliver, the defensive coach at Alabama, does a super job of game-planning on pass plays, and he likes to use eight backs in pass coverage.

Coach Oliver did an outstanding job, and I had made a mistake by trying to throw on third downs to Kirk because they had him completely covered.

Our defense kept us in the game. We were behind only 7-0 at halftime. At that point our guys didn't feel real bad, and we hadn't lost our poise.

We had some pretty good emotion going in the dressing room. This was a good sign that our players were starting to understand the point we coaches had been making for months: Just keep playing hard the entire game, forget how the breaks are going, and something good will happen for us.

That is the way winners play, and the Gators' halftime attitude showed that maybe they could learn to do it. But it was only halftime, and we still needed to beat a good team to prove to ourselves we were winners.

In the second half we got behind 10-0 with about 11 minutes remaining in the third quarter, but I was pleased that our team kept its poise and confidence. Then we put together a drive: Shane Matthews hit a few passes and suddenly we were inside the Alabama 10-yard line.

From there Shane had to scramble out to his right, and Terence Barber drifted across the back of the end zone just as he was supposed to do in this situation. They made a wonderful throw and catch for a touchdown that made it 10-7. Gosh, what a relief. I'd been starting to wonder if we would ever score that day.

This was early September in Alabama, and it was stifling hot. Sweat was pouring off everyone. This game was going to come down to a test of wills and conditioning. I was very relieved that we were back in the game; we were determined that our team was not going to come up short.

Alabama put a drive together, and it got to be about third-and-five. Their quarterback, Gary Hollingsworth, had a tendency to drop back and look at his main receiver pretty much all the way. Jim Bates, our defensive coordinator, had told safety Will White to watch for that.

Will, who had the game of his life that day with three interceptions and several key tackles, followed Hollingsworth's eyes and came off the hash in a two-deep zone to make a sprinting interception on our own two-yard line. Just a wonderful play.

I sort of wished he had caught it in the end zone so we'd start out on our 20 but, anyway, he made a beautiful play, and we got the ball first-and-10 on our own two-yard line.

At that point I told Shane and Ernie Mills, our talented wide receiver, to go with the 14-pass-Z, which calls for Ernie to run an outside route. To tell you the truth, I think on the way out onto the field Shane told Ernie to run an inside streak instead of an outside.

It's amazing how some of these big plays happen. On the series before, Alabama's starting free safety had gotten banged up a little bit and wasn't in the game. An inside streak ended up being a post pattern, and Alabama had a substitute free safety for coverage.

Bama was in a three-deep zone and their defensive back did not get back in position the way he should have. Ernie ran right past the defensive cornerback and the free safety. Shane dropped back and threw the ball about as far as he could, hitting him on dead stride. After the catch, Ernie made it all the way to the Alabama 30-yard line.

Though we didn't get a touchdown on that possession, we got close enough for Arden Czyzewski to boot a field goal, tying the game 10-10.

We had hung in there and suddenly it was starting to look pretty good. Our defense was playing well; they played well the entire game. We felt we could win it at that point. Even though our offense didn't score a touchdown the rest of the game, we moved the ball, we made some first downs, and we were able to keep Alabama in their own territory, where our defense played just superbly.

Assistant coach Bob Sanders is a punt-blocking guru for us. He studies the tapes, and we have had outstanding success at blocking punts under his direction. He felt all week that we could block an Alabama punt. We worked hard on it.

Late in the game Alabama had to punt from around their own 15. Coach Sanders felt Alabama's punter Stan Moss had been taking too long in taking his steps and punting the ball.

So he told Jimmy Spencer to go for the block. Jimmy was very good coming around the corner and timing it right to block a kick. He rushed in there and blocked Moss' punt, and a bunch of guys played jump ball and tipped it around until defensive back Richard Fain recovered it in the end zone for a touchdown.

After that, Alabama had a little drive, which resulted in a field goal to make it 17-13. We were trying to run out the clock. On second-and-11, Shane hit receiver Tre Everett on a curl pattern, and Tre turned and ran upfield and then ran out of bounds right in front of our bench.

I grabbed him and asked what in the world he was doing; we were trying to run out the clock and win the game. Tre really didn't understand.

Later Tre told me why: "Coach Spurrier, that's the first time in my life I've ever been in a position to stay in bounds and put the game away and win it." It was something new for Tre, something new for the Gators, to go to Tuscaloosa and beat an outstanding Alabama team, preserving the victory under pressure.

Our 8,000 fans stayed right to the end. Our players were high-fiving as they left the field, and many of them went over to the end zone section to celebrate with those loyal fans who had made the trip and sat in that wilting heat to cheer us on.

Carl Franks, who coaches our running backs and has been with me as a player or coach most of the time since 1980, jogged along with me to the dressing room. He said, "Coach, I don't know if I've ever seen you this emotional after a victory."

I told Carl he might be right, that I was so excited because this game had shattered the barriers that held back the Florida Gators. Our players now knew they could beat a quality opponent, beat the best teams in the SEC, and now we would expect to do it.

I really believe that mentally that day we passed into uncharted waters for Florida football, going into unknown territory where we know we can beat good teams and have a chance to win the championship.

Shoot, I thought, we've got a good chance now – we've got a good chance to win it all this year. Little did I know what was waiting in the wings the following week from the NCAA and the SEC: that these innocent players would be stripped of a chance to win the official championship and would have to settle for trying to become No. 1 in the conference.

In the dressing room players were hugging each other, coaches were hugging players. It was a game that set the tone for Florida football for the next two years.

Sportswriter Bill King covered the game for the *Gainesville Sun*, and he wrote in the next day's newspaper that it "looked, smelled and tasted a lot like the games that had left them alone and depressed in years past. ... It was another one of those familiar afternoons for the Gators ... only this time ... Florida reversed field on its own history and walked away with a victory."

I think that was the most exciting part of the victory. We came from 10 points behind in the second half at Alabama and made the big plays to win. Then the players realized, hey, if we play hard the entire game and play smart, we'll have a chance. And I believe they really gained confidence in the coaching staff also.

You know, it's easy to talk about being successful and to say this is what we've got to do, but until you've actually experienced the success, you don't know that you can do it.

So, in that game, the Gators threw out that bad habit of losing the crucial games. Since then, in the past two seasons, we've proven that we have learned how to win the big ones.

That is why, without a doubt, I look back and see the Alabama game of 1990 as the turning point in our success at Florida over these championship seasons.

6

ROCKY TOP THRASHING

For each game on our schedule, we assign an assistant coach to take charge of preparing us for that specific opponent. As part of his duties, the assistant gives the scouting report to the team on Monday night of game week and talks to the team in the pregame meeting.

Jim Bates, our defensive coordinator, was assigned the Tennessee game in 1990. He had coached at Tennessee the year before and knew their personnel. I will never forget his Monday night report.

Coach Bates told the team: "Fellas, this is a great football team we're playing in Knoxville. Their two offensive tackles [Charles McRae and Antoine Davis] are going to be first-round NFL draft choices. They've got two of the best defensive ends in the nation [Chuckie Smith and Chris Mims], probably the best receiver [Carl Pickens] and a great quarterback [Andy Kelly]."

He went on to relate that the Vols had an outstanding kicking game and excellent running backs, that their fans would be going absolutely crazy and that Neyland Stadium would be incredibly loud, with over 95,000 people there.

Coach Bates concluded, "This is probably the best team you'll ever play against."

I almost interrupted Jim to say: "Wait a minute, Coach. If all that's true, then we don't have a chance." However, after collecting my thoughts, I told them, "They are good players, Coach Bates, but we do have a chance if we go up there and play hard and well."

Jim agreed with me. He had pumped up the Vols' strengths pretty good to impress our team. When we played them, we did find out that talent-wise they were the best team we were to play in 1990. In fact, they were probably the best team we played in 1991, too.

And Coach Bates, who is now an outstanding assistant coach in the NFL, turned out to be a prophet on the future draft status of several Vols. The offensive tackles, Davis and McRae, were both first-round picks, and the two defensive ends, Smith and Mims, went the following year, one in the first round and the other in the second.

The game was a madhouse by kickoff time, but it was reassuring to see thousands of Gators there in their orange and blue. Many of our followers had been in Knoxville most of the week, touring the area, going to Gatlinburg and seeing all the sights in that beautiful mountain area.

We were ready to play, but we just couldn't execute on offense. Tennessee was ahead only 7-3 at halftime, but our offense was going nowhere. We had a very difficult time blocking their right defensive end, and he was disrupting everything we tried to do to move the ball. Our left tackle had his hands full, from the first snap from scrimmage until his last play before we put him on the bench.

Our game plan was not good. Early in the game, we tried to throw the ball too much instead of running it, and we dug ourselves into a hole. Still, at halftime we were very much in the game.

We reviewed what we wanted done at halftime, and our players were upbeat and encouraged. We had dropped a touchdown pass, then lost an almost-certain touchdown return on an interception when a teammate bumped into Will White while trying to block. Still, we were within four points. We came out for the second half fired up and confident that things were going to be fine.

How quickly one play can change the course of a game.

Tennessee's Dale Carter, an All-American defensive back, grabbed the second-half kickoff at the nine-yard line. It looked like the ball was going to go out of bounds and, at that moment, we were glad he'd caught it there near the sideline.

Then all of a sudden he went up the sideline and reversed his field. When one of our starting defensive backs, Monty Grow, got a piece of him at about the 50, Carter shook him off and sprinted in for a touchdown.

We ran the next kickoff out to midfield, and our bench came alive. Then we made a first down, and you could feel the momentum swinging back our way. But seconds later, Errict Rhett lost a fumble on second-and-two.

They got the ball and, taking advantage of the turnover, moved rapidly to a score. It came on a tight-end-around pass, thrown perfectly to Pickens, who was just a half-step behind defensive back Jimmy Spencer.

On the next play we turned the ball back over to Tennessee. They scored again. Suddenly it was 28-3, and the place was rocking. Bedlam set in on the Tennessee sideline and in the stands. Our halftime confidence had evaporated.

Quarterback Shane Matthews had a very long night. We couldn't protect him, and I thought at this point we needed to go ahead and put in the reserves.

I remembered reading a book called *Leadership Secrets of Attila The Hun*, in which Attila's philosophy is spelled out: "When defeat is inevitable and there is no way to win, retreat, pull back and save your troops for another battle."

I felt at that point in the third quarter we had no chance to win. Defeat was inevitable. We couldn't pass-block and therefore didn't have time to throw and give ourselves a chance to get back in the game.

The stadium was brimming over with enthusiasm, providing even more momentum for the Tennessee team. They were an extremely talented group of athletes playing at the top of their game, and there was no way that would change on this night.

So I considered what positives we could possibly get out of the game at this point: We could avoid getting key players hurt in a futile cause, and we could look at younger players and see how they react and perform at this level of competition.

That's what we did. We pulled back and gave everyone an opportunity to play. Perhaps that decision contributed to the final 45-3 margin, but again the Vols were in such total control that the game might have gotten that bad anyhow.

It did help our team for the future. We saw some things in several of the young players that encouraged us to give them more playing time, and they responded as the season went along. I especially wanted to see Brian Fox and Kyle Morris play quarterback in competition against an outstanding team.

We were looking for answers; one that came out of this game was that, without question, Shane Matthews was our best quarterback. He's a smart young man who doesn't make the real critical bad play that beats his own team.

I believe sticking with Shane through the Auburn-Georgia-Kentucky-FSU stretch the rest of the season solidified our team at quarterback and was very instrumental in the success that came after the loss at Tennessee. From that point through the end of the championship year of 1991 we won 10 consecutive conference games.

Even though we were soundly trounced, the Tennessee game made us better coaches. We became a much better team after that game because we needed to make personnel changes to improve, and the correct changes were made.

Ironically, that game probably hurt Tennessee. Neyland Stadium was like a morgue during their game against Alabama the next week. Nobody was yelling or screaming; it appeared the Vols had spent so much emotion against us they didn't have much left for Alabama, their longtime bitter rival. Alabama beat Tennessee in a game of five field goals, 9-6.

After the season, I asked Coach Majors about that game and the Vols' apparent lack of emotion. He said, "You're right. Nothing happened that day to excite our fans." He also said Neyland Stadium on the night Tennessee played Florida was the loudest he had heard it in all his years of playing and coaching there.

I know one thing – they played "Rocky Top" about as many times as they could in one night, and their fans loved giving us a good tail-kicking.

For our team, thinking about the Tennessee game was painful from the moment the game ended until we kicked it off against them the next year in Gainesville.

I'm a firm believer that any loss hurts, but sometimes getting whipped soundly is more beneficial to your team than a heart-breaking close loss. With a heartbreaker, you have a tendency to point fingers: "If he'd made that play, or if I'd made that call. ..." You're looking at the little things that made the difference between winning and losing.

But if you're beaten soundly, everyone accepts the blame; if you have the right kind of people, you begin to think about how you can get better.

We had the right kind of people, and we got much better in 1990.

7

AUBURN/GEORGIA
ISN'T ONE GAME

O ver the years, the heart of Florida's football schedule has
been the annual back-to-back games against Auburn and
Georgia. Often the two-week stretch begins Halloween
weekend, which perhaps is appropriate: The horror stories of
ruined seasons and lost championships are certainly part of
Gator football tradition, and each succeeding group of players
has gone into these two weeks as if they were carrying past failures on their shoulders.

Soon after accepting the head coaching job at Florida, I started hearing from Gator fans who were concerned about playing
these two traditional games against our oldest rivals on succes-
sive Saturdays. They told me in person, by letter and in tele-
phone calls that we just can't play them that way; that it was
impossible to get the team up two weeks in a row for games of
that magnitude. To them, Auburn/Georgia was one game, with
the Gators facing two foes at once.

I would tell them, now, wait a minute – we're not the only team
in America that has two difficult, traditional games back to back.
The most obvious example, of course, is Georgia, which faces

Florida and then Auburn. In 1990 and 1991 Tennessee had to face the Gators one week and Alabama the next.

If we can't get excited about playing Auburn and Georgia, our two oldest rivals, then something is wrong with us; we shouldn't use the schedule as an excuse for losing. Certainly we have a good chance to beat one or both of these teams each year.

This is our schedule; this is who we play. If we're not good enough, not tough enough or not smart enough, let's say so; but let's not look for excuses because we play two quality opponents back to back. That's just part of playing football.

In the 1990 season, we got trounced by Tennessee on the way to the Auburn and Georgia showdowns. Fortunately, we had a team with character, and Akron as our Homecoming opponent the week after Tennessee. We beat Akron 59-0 in a game we used for regrouping and practicing. Auburn was next.

During the off-week between the Akron and Auburn games, we had two or three good practices and a solid scrimmage on Saturday morning before the players went home. We were talking all week about Auburn, Georgia and Kentucky, the three conference games.

We needed to put together a three-game winning streak to finish first in the conference. We knew that because Alabama had already beaten Tennessee, and everyone had had at least one loss or worse. In fact, Tennessee was leading the conference with a loss and a tie.

Our team understood that if we won the last three, the Gators would win the conference championship, although we would not be officially recognized.

In 1989, the NCAA looked into allegations against Galen Hall and the Gator football program. The NCAA determined that in 1986, Hall had provided a child support payment for a member of the football squad. Hall and the player, who was a junior, denied this allegation, but Florida was found guilty anyway. The NCAA imposed sanctions that would not allow Florida's 1990 team to go to a bowl game. Because of an SEC rule barring a team that is ineligible for a bowl game from being declared the official SEC champion, the Gators could not officially be recognized as 1990 SEC champions.

But winning the championship was our goal before the season and certainly that's what we were trying to do. Right after that scrimmage on Saturday of the off-week, I started talking to the team about Auburn, and only about Auburn.

I told our players that from now on and through the end of the Auburn game, we were going to be thinking and talking only about Auburn, talking about how Auburn stole one from them the year before on the last play of the game on fourth down and 26 yards to go, thinking about how Auburn's fans threw whiskey bottles at them from the stands after the game.

We were going to be talking about what we would need to do to beat Auburn. In 1990 they were coming to our place to play three weeks after Tennessee had demolished us. I remember how Jack Hairston of the *Gainesville Sun* said that if the Gators got behind early it could be a blowout, just like the Tennessee game. He meant the Gators might get blown out, not Auburn.

A lot of the writers were picking Auburn. They were ranked fourth in the nation, and a couple of teams ahead of them had lost earlier in the day; so it was possible that night for them to move to number one. However, although they had tied Tennessee earlier in the year, Auburn had not been playing extremely well, and several of the games they had won had been close.

It was a game our players really wanted. That touchdown pass the year before on fourth-and-26 had beaten them 10-7, and the barrage of whiskey bottles followed seconds later. All of our players remembered that game vividly, and they wanted to get back at Auburn.

One of the Auburn players, who was from Lakeland, Florida, had been quoted in one of the papers as saying that when the Gators get behind, they quit. That was a quote that really fired up our players. It was one we had posted on the locker room wall and put on the lockers of all the players the day of the game.

It was the kind of game where we wanted to beat Auburn as badly as we could, if we could. Sometimes if you win by one point, that's fine. But if you're good enough to beat a team by three or four touchdowns, then I believe that's what you should try to do. We try to score as much as we can without doing something unnecessary to run up the score, like calling timeout at the end of the game.

Auburn came to Gainesville and worked out in our stadium Friday afternoon. I'll tell you what was sort of funny:

While Auburn was working out, Coach Pat Dye sent one of his administrative staff over to our equipment men to tell them he wanted to say hello to me after their practice back in the tunnel leading to their dressing room.

I had just finished a meeting with our quarterbacks and receivers, and had just finished telling the guys that we were going to use the screen back to the quarterback. That's a play in which Shane Matthews takes the ball and throws it out sideways to a wide receiver, who throws it back to Shane. It was a play we scored on against Kentucky in 1991.

I told them we were going to use it against Auburn because we hadn't used it all season. We had been working on it, though, so it was all set up, and I felt very good about its chances.

So when I went out to the tunnel to greet Coach Dye and his wife, Sue, the first thing he said to me was, "Steve, are you going to use that screen back to the quarterback tomorrow?"

I said, "Coach, of course we are. How did you know?"

Then I remembered that one of his assistant coaches, Wayne Bolt, had come from Clemson and had coached against my Duke teams. The week of a game any assistant coach who has past experience against the opposing coach will tell their current head coach about all the old trick plays.

Coach Bolt knew about the little dipsy-do plays and told Coach Dye he needed to watch out for one of them, the screen back to the quarterback.

It all worked out fine: We didn't use that play that night, and used it in a later game for a touchdown. We had them looking for all kinds of trick stuff all night. As it turned out, however, we didn't use any trick plays.

Another one of the interesting aspects leading up to the Auburn game and the remainder of our season was that after getting blown out by Tennessee, every sportswriter I know completely wrote us off as having a chance to finish first in the SEC.

They said Florida looked like a bunch of fools for wanting to appeal the NCAA sanctions because they weren't going to win the SEC and would have given up scholarships and mortgaged the future. The Gators, they said, didn't have a chance because they were blown out at Tennessee.

It was as though it were all over because we had one loss. And history tells us that any school with a 6-1 record has a great chance of winning or tying for the conference championship. The last unbeaten team in the conference was in 1983, when Auburn was 6-0. There hadn't been an unbeaten team with seven conference wins since Alabama in 1977.

The Auburn game was one in which our team was fired up and the Tigers were pretty much ready to play, too. They had a lot to play for, with the chance to jump to number one in the nation that night with a convincing win. But, of course, we had a lot to play for also.

The game began with us not doing much on our first three possessions. We did absolutely nothing consistently on offense except go backward. But our defense completely stuffed Auburn and set the tone for the night.

Auburn got the ball at or near midfield three or four times early, but could not score or really put a dent in our defense. Finally, on about our fourth possession, Shane went back and hit Ernie Mills on a beautiful corner throw. On the next play Shane got sacked for a four- or five-yard loss.

At second-and-about-15 we called a play that we use often – the flanker, from an inside position, running a corner route – and we caught Auburn in the perfect coverage for the play to work.

They had put in a new coverage to use against us to try to stop the throw over the middle. What they did was send one safety running immediately to the middle of the field to take that pass away, and then one safety running deep in the middle, making it a defense that's very strong if you are throwing over the middle.

However, it's very weak if you're throwing a corner route because it's man-to-man coverage, and the defensive back has no help on the outside. Ernie ran a beautiful corner route, Shane made an excellent throw and we got a 25- to 30-yard gain down to about the 15-yard line.

Auburn did not call that defense the rest of the game. Coach Dye is pretty much a conservative, fundamental-type coach, and he does not like a lot of new gimmick defensive plays, or a lot of new gimmick offensive plays, for that matter.

I'll bet he told the defensive coaches that's the last time he wanted to see that coverage.

That is his coaching philosophy, and he has been very successful. I really respect Coach Dye and everything he has done coaching the Auburn team. He has won several championships and has sort of been the top dog in the conference.

Anyhow, after that pass completion we went on to score on a short run by Willie McClendon, who scored three touchdowns that night. We did not throw a touchdown pass in that game. Interestingly, the only other game in which we didn't throw a touchdown pass was the 45-3 loss to Tennessee three weeks earlier.

We scored 24 points in the second quarter against Auburn to lead 34-7 at halftime. I think what really inspired our fans that night was when Auburn had the ball at midfield with 40 seconds remaining in the half and failed to convert on fourth-and-five. We moved the ball in three plays, one a big pass over the middle to Kirk Kirkpatrick, and Arden Czyzewski kicked a 38-yard field goal as time expired.

Scoring just before the half always picks up a crowd. It seemed like our fans had never seen that happen before. In the past, most teams, and not only Florida teams, who get a lead don't want to do anything stupid to give the other team a chance.

But I believe you've got to keep pushing, you have to keep trying to score all the way through the game. Certainly you don't want to do anything to hurt yourself, but again you've got to let your players keep pushing and pushing and trying to score.

That was our last game at Florida Field in 1990, and that field goal right before the half brought the crowd noise in the stadium up to a level that I hadn't heard before.

We really controlled the game in the second half. Errict Rhett ran for well over 100 yards in the game. He had a beautiful run on a draw play of about 38 to 40 yards for a touchdown, and we beat them pretty good – 48-7 – and it really gave our players tremendous confidence that we were a good team and we could play with anybody.

The terrible outing in Knoxville was history, but a game we had learned from to help us with the big win against Auburn.

There's no doubt our victory over Auburn was a big one, but immediately after the game it was time to talk about Georgia and how important it would be to knock down one of those old barriers that surrounded Florida football by beating these two teams back to back.

8

GEORGIA COMES FIRST

All games are important to all coaches, but certainly there are one or two each year that stand out; and if you had your choice of one victory, well ... which one would it be?

For me, since coming to Florida as head coach and remembering my days as a player and an alumnus, it would be a victory over Georgia.

As a player, one of the most memorable losses I've ever had came in 1966, when we went to Jacksonville with a 7-0 record and a chance to win the first SEC championship in school history. We played pretty well in the first half, although we had only a 10-3 lead because we failed to score when we had some chances.

In the second half Georgia just steamrolled us; they blitzed, and we couldn't pick them up. They ran the ball very well and just absolutely controlled the game to beat us 27-10.

That loss knocked us out of the championship race and out of a chance to finish with a very high national ranking.

We ended up with a 9-2 record after an upset loss to Miami, which wasn't even a Top 20 team.

As a Florida alumnus, the past 25 years or so I've endured the frustration and anger Gators feel over losses to Georgia and the manner in which some of them occurred. Georgia has beaten Florida something like 11 or 12 times when the conference championship was on the line.

Florida beat Georgia in 1984 when the Gators were in position to win the championship, which they later did. However, that title was taken away the following May because of violations of NCAA rules by the coaching staff in the early 1980s.

So, it certainly was a very emotional moment for me to compete against Georgia as a head coach for the first time in 1990 because of how often they had beaten us in the past. I really feel like we have just as good a group of players as Georgia does, and there is no reason why we shouldn't do well against them every year.

Immediately after the 48-7 victory over Auburn, I told the team in the locker room that the Georgia game was one every Gator wants to win, and that we were going to be ready for the Bulldogs.

I said it was a big advantage for us to play Georgia in Jacksonville. We get on a bus for a short ride, and they catch an airplane. The game is played on Florida soil in a stadium named the Gator Bowl. There would be no excuses from us about having to play two tough opponents in a row or having to play in Jacksonville, where Florida teams historically have not done well.

To me, everything points to the fact that we have a little bit of an advantage over Georgia by playing in the Gator Bowl in Jacksonville, Florida, each year. It would be like the University of Florida going to Atlanta, Georgia, every season to play Georgia in a stadium named the Bulldog Bowl. We'd have to fly to Atlanta but they would just bus over from Athens, and so forth.

The week of the game the newspaper write-ups were about how Florida was favored as usual but that it didn't mean anything – it hadn't meant anything in the past. Many of the writers also noted how seldom the Gators beat Auburn and Georgia back to back, and talked about the victory margin former Georgia coach Vince Dooley had over Florida.

Ray Goff, now the Bulldogs' head coach, said he'd been to that game for 15 years or more, and that Florida usually had the best team, but that hadn't ever mattered to the Georgia players – they found a way to win.

We found some clippings from the 1989 game, in which Georgia had beaten Florida 17-10. Several of their players had said something along the lines of, "We just want it more than the Florida players do." So, we had a lot of reasons to be emotionally charged up.

The Georgia team of 1990 was not very good. They had struggled some and were playing a lot of young players. They ended with a 5-6 record that year.

Our week of practice was outstanding. We told our team that the only way we could lose this game in 1990 was if we simply were not tough enough to win it. We were more talented, definitely more talented. We just had too much going for us, and we would not lose unless we fell on our face. Unless we ourselves stumbled, Georgia was not capable of beating us.

By Friday our team was ready to play Georgia. I mean, really ready to play Georgia.

I usually call on Gene Ellenson, a former assistant head coach at Florida when I played in the 1960s, to talk to the team before one game a year. I believe that if you pick out one game to bring in a coach who hasn't talked to the team all year, you get a little bit of an emotional edge or advantage from it.

Coach Ellenson has been speaking with my teams once a year since 1987, when I became head coach at Duke University. So, we called on him for the Georgia game; I had told him it was his game before the season started.

The night before the game Coach Ellenson said, "Steve, how much do you believe I need to say to these guys?" I said, "Coach, I'm going to tell you the truth: They're ready to play. We're ready to beat Georgia, so you don't really need to do a whole bunch."

He could sense it also. He could sense that here was a team that had played well against Auburn and was confident and ready to play just as well this week.

Our players were very quiet on the bus ride over from Gainesville. They were very quiet at dinner Friday night. We allowed them to watch a movie in their rooms after dinner and then they came back for a snack at 9:30. That was when Coach Ellenson gave his talk.

Basically, he didn't give a long, involved, emotional talk as he's so very capable of doing because he thought this team was really ready to play. I thought the talk was just perfect. Our players were already anxious, they were ready for Georgia.

Our players had gotten sick and tired of hearing about how the Georgia players wanted it more than they did, how they were tougher than the Florida players, how Georgia players would fight to the end, and so forth. With the frame of mind our team was in, the time was right to take on Georgia.

Playing Georgia in the Gator Bowl is an exciting experience. You drive in on the team bus through the fans of both teams – dressed in orange and blue, and in red and black – and they are all worked up about the game, some of them too much. You look at all these people at their cookouts, tailgating, with barbs being thrown back and forth, and it makes you happy to be part of it, Gator or Bulldog.

Looking around as we neared the stadium that Saturday, I thought about how tough it must be for the police force with the overwhelming mass of people and vehicles converging into the area. Jacksonville city officials work hard to make the Florida-Georgia game an efficient operation, and I'm certain it is a difficult task. I think they do an excellent job.

It was a relief to get the team buses parked and to head toward the locker room. It's a madhouse before you even get inside the stadium. Fans from both sides are everywhere, and you walk a gauntlet of people who want to encourage you, discourage you or just observe.

We had our team in the locker room as soon as possible and started the normal pregame process. It didn't take long for us to walk out into an arena that many of our players had never experienced, and probably would not forget.

This game is a true college football classic. The stadium is divided almost 50-50 between those wearing orange and blue and those wearing red and black, and tickets are very hard to come by.

After our pregame warmup we went back to the locker room, and Jerry Anderson, our assistant head coach who was a teammate of mine, gave an emotional talk just before we went back onto the field.

Though we scored three touchdowns and a field goal in the first half, we had the ball inside the Georgia 20-yard line five times without scoring. Shane Matthews fumbled on the one-yard line on a poor exchange with the center, we lost a fumble at the 16, we went for a first down on fourth-and-one and didn't make it, we missed a 35-yard field goal attempt and then as the half ended we lost a great scoring opportunity.

We let the clock die right at the end of the first half: Shane had one of those plays where he was supposed to throw the ball into the end zone, or maybe get the first down, but he ended up dumping it off to the tight end, who gained about five yards as time expired with us at their 13-yard line. We couldn't even kick a field goal.

We had played well enough that we were ahead 24-7 at that time, but if we had been really sharp we could have had 50 points at halftime. Obviously, Georgia's defense dug in and came up with some big plays.

Early in the third quarter we used a play we'd never run before. Shane threw a little pitch to Errict Rhett, who handed it back to him. Terence Barber, our wide receiver, got completely behind the Georgia free safety for a 51-yard touchdown. It put us up 31-7 and really put the game away.

Our defense was sensational. I believe Georgia had to punt about 11 times, and they did not make a first down in either the second or third quarters. Huey Richardson, Mark Murray, Godfrey Myles, Richard Fain, Jerry Odom and Tim Paulk had outstanding performances.

The final score was 38-7. It was a total victory, the biggest margin of victory for the Gators over the Bulldogs in the history of this series, which dates back to 1915. The 1952 Florida team had beaten Georgia 30-0 for the previous largest spread.

Some of the Georgia players said later that we had run up the score, but that was not true. Our reserves played most of the final quarter, and once the margin got to 31-7 early in the third quarter, we only scored one more touchdown – none in the final quarter.

What made me proudest about the way our players performed against Georgia was their reaction to our not scoring in the first half on the five trips inside their 20-yard line. Our team didn't panic or hang their heads. In fact, there was total confidence that it was only a matter of time – if they kept playing hard, the points, and the win, would come.

I thought a quote from Mark Murray, our fine senior defensive end, in the *Palm Beach Post* the next day did a good job of summing up what we hoped the players' attitude would be that Saturday and in Saturdays to come:

"It's just what we learned all year long from Coach Spurrier," he said. "Good things and bad things will happen, but just accept them and keep playing. We're more confident knowing that if we get down in the game, we can still do it. I think in the past we second-guessed ourselves."

I always felt we had the upper hand, that we were the better team out there, and as long as we didn't panic, we'd be OK. It's nice to have the players thinking that way, too, especially against Georgia.

This Florida team shattered a barrier which had haunted some of the finest teams in our history. Four times Gator teams had entered the Georgia game with seven wins and all four teams lost. That included my 1966 team and the teams in 1974, 1975 and 1985.

The mystique Georgia held over Florida in Jacksonville ended November 10, 1990.

We were now two games through the three-game winning streak we had talked about. Certainly they were the toughest two games during this stretch, but the road to becoming No. 1 in the conference now headed toward Kentucky. As soon as the Georgia game was over, it was time to talk with the team about Kentucky. We were on the verge of proving wrong all those people who kept saying the Gators couldn't do it.

After we received the NCAA sanctions in September, Gerald Ensley of the *Tallahassee Democrat* wrote, "If tomorrow brings word that Steve Spurrier and John Lombardi are going to attempt to fly naked off the top of the Century Tower at the University of Florida, it will be no surprise. Because the Gator head football coach and university president have gone daffy in their distress over the NCAA sanctions handed on Sept. 20." He was referring to our talking about appealing the NCAA sanctions.

We did appeal the sanctions against players who had nothing to do with the alleged violation in 1986, and offered to take a future scholarship reduction in exchange for giving these inno-cent players a chance to compete for the championship.

However, Ensley wrote that Florida is just an average 6-5 team, and that there is no way the Gators are going to win the SEC. They've still got Tennessee, Auburn and Georgia left, and at best they will be 6-5 and maybe get an invitation to the Peach Bowl, he wrote.

This was the attitude of many people around the country: that the Gators could not finish first. We were picked fourth in the SEC by members of the news media who cover the conference teams. Only one sportswriter, Mike Fleming of the *The Commercial-Appeal* in Memphis picked us to finish number one in the SEC in 1990, and I appreciate Mike giving us that vote of confidence.

I always get a little extra bit of emotion when I coach against Bill Curry, Kentucky's coach. After Pepper Rodgers was fired at Georgia Tech in 1979, Curry succeeded him as head coach. I was a member of Rodgers' staff that '79 season.

I had just bought a new house in Marietta, just outside of Atlanta, and had three small children; certainly I was looking forward to staying at Tech, coaching the quarterbacks and maybe becoming offensive coordinator.

Bill came in and felt he needed to bring a lot of new coaches in, and that he needed to interview some other people for the quarterback coaching position. I like Bill Curry, but still I wasn't good enough to work for him back in 1980. Fortunately, when I was left off the new staff at Georgia Tech, one of the biggest breaks of my coaching career came my way when Red Wilson gave me the opportunity to come to Duke University as offensive coordinator and to install my ideas of offensive football.

The game of football is an emotional sport, and I want to show Bill Curry I can coach. So I certainly get a little more excited going into a contest against him.

On Friday before the Kentucky game we were up there in Lexington jogging around in Commonwealth Stadium. Everybody was fairly relaxed, throwing the ball around and going over assignments. It was a normal Friday practice.

A back-up defensive back, Kurt Young of Tampa, strolled past me on the field and said, "Coach, this season is turning out just like you thought it would, isn't it?"

I answered, "Well, Kurt, I didn't know for sure, but I knew we had a good chance for this to happen."

It was a nice compliment because he sensed that we, as coaches, were aware of what could happen, had expected it to happen all along and had gotten the players to believe that we were going to finish on top of the SEC.

Our governor-elect, Lawton Chiles, came by the hotel Friday night. He was in Lexington to attend a governor's conference, and he gave our team a nice little talk the night before the game. It was nice to see him and lieutenant governor-elect Buddy MacKay there.

The weather cooperated with us on this trip to Lexington. I

had heard some of the horror stories about past Gator trips to Kentucky, but at kickoff it was about 60 degrees and the sun was shining. In fact, it was so comfortable that I coached the game in a light sweater vest over a short-sleeved shirt.

The game started out a little bit tough. Shane got thrown for a safety early in the game, and we were behind 2-0. Kentucky felt they had to blitz and take their chances, so Shane took some heavy losses early, including the safety.

When they hit him in the end zone, we had a pass called in which our blocking scheme didn't allow for an outside line-backer, and the 25-second clock was running down on Shane before he could change the play.

Even though we were on our own one-yard line, Shane felt he needed to go ahead and snap the ball. Later on I said to him, "If you're ever stuck on your own one-yard line, they can only penalize you one-half yard for delay of game. Then, if we're on the half-yard line, they can only penalize you a quarter of a yard. So don't worry about the clock if you're stuck down there."

I hope that was a good learning experience for him. He hasn't made that mistake since.

Godfrey Myles, one of our finest senior leaders that year, picked off a pass and ran it for a touchdown to get us a 7-2 lead, but then they hit a 73-yard screen pass for a score to put them up at 9-7 at the end of the first quarter.

I found out that Kentucky football fans can scream and holler. They were screaming pretty well there for a while, and it appeared to help their team.

But the second quarter was our best quarter in 1990. We scored 24 on Kentucky in that quarter. Receiver Ernie Mills, another fine senior leader, got man-to-man coverage when they blitzed and he caught a pair of touchdown passes on corner routes.

Right at the end of the half we got the ball at our 20 with a minute left on the clock. We were ahead 28-9, but we went with the no-huddle offense, and tight end Kirk Kirkpatrick, yet anoth-er great senior leader, made a couple of big catches. We had a TD pass go right off the hands of a receiver right before time expired, so we just kicked a field goal to make it 31-9. That gave us some pretty good momentum.

In the second half we came out strong. Errict Rhett ran for more than 100 yards, and Willie McClendon ran very well, too. I think they combined for more than 200 yards rushing, and Shane threw for more than 300 yards. Our defense was outstanding and, with our reserves playing a lot of minutes, the final score was 47-15.

I told our players of a tradition we had started at Duke: If we won the conference championship, we were going to have a picture taken of the entire team underneath the scoreboard. We gathered at the scoreboard at Commonwealth Stadium and had a team picture taken so our guys could remember finishing first in the SEC in 1990 for the rest of their lives.

We had an excellent following of Gators up there. Some 4,000 to 5,000 fans went to Kentucky to watch us finish first, and they stayed to the very end – even for the photo session under the scoreboard. It seemed like there were more Gators than Wildcats there at the end of the game.

We were number one in the SEC, but we couldn't be called the champions. The NCAA Infractions Committee had felt they had to punish Florida, although there was only one alleged violation, because the rules say that if a violation occurs within five years of a previous violation, then sanctions must be imposed on a school.

The committee thought they had given us a light punishment. They thought we were going to be a 7-4 team, a team that didn't have a chance to win the championship and earn the Sugar Bowl berth and official title.

The reason the penalty seemed so severe was that it punished our players more for becoming an excellent team. It punished them more because they had made a commitment to be the best they could be. They lifted weights harder than they ever had in their lives, they were in better running shape than they had ever been and they had set goals to achieve.

The NCAA actually punished them for working that hard and becoming that good, for making the commitment to be their very best and living up to it. That is something that will always bother me. The punishment was directed strictly at the kids on that team who had no violations and had nothing to do with what happened in the past. That's why I wanted the punishment to be removed from them and applied in another area.

When it happened we talked to the team about changing our goals just slightly. Instead of talking about winning a championship we talked about being number one in the SEC. We still had our goal of winning 10 games, which we didn't reach, and of finishing in the Top 10, which we did.

The way I look at that situation now, I would tell those players, "You were the conference champions, but you were not recognized. The SEC didn't recognize you and never will, but you know in your minds and hearts that you won the championship that year."

I can assure everyone that the emotion I had there in Lexington in 1990 was just like it was when Duke beat North Carolina for the ACC championship in 1989, and when we beat Kentucky in 1991 to win the "official" SEC championship.

After we beat Kentucky in 1990 we had a week off before we played FSU. I think, as coaches, we allowed our players to celebrate too much. We normally talk about celebrating a victory that night, and the next day start focusing on the next opponent. After beating Kentucky and finishing first, I believe we all, including myself, relaxed a little too much, and we didn't quite get the edge back for the FSU game.

FSU had a season that wasn't a great one for them because of their high expectations. Miami beat them pretty good, and Auburn beat them in Alabama, so they came into our game 8-2 and we went in 9-1.

They had played a lackluster game against Memphis State in Orlando's Florida Citrus Bowl. While we were having an emotional time in Lexington, the FSU players and coaches were probably not even smiling in the locker room after the Memphis State game.

They definitely were ready for us. You could tell they were all thinking about the Gators on that game night in Tallahassee. FSU played very well, and Coach Bobby Bowden called a beautiful game.

FSU quarterback Casey Weldon hit a big pass to Lawrence Dawsey, an extremely talented and tough receiver, for an early touchdown. He hit key third-down plays all night, and Amp Lee's running was exceptional. We had almost 500 yards of offense, and we had a chance to score more than the 30 points we got. We had one touchdown called back because of a delay-of-game infraction. FSU won by a final score of 45-30.

It's always tough to lose to FSU, but maybe we learned something. We just weren't quite ready to go 10-1. We learned you can't celebrate until all 11 games are over. Maybe that loss to FSU in '90 really helped our team in 1991. The situation in '91 was similar, as far as our beating Kentucky for the conference championship and then having to come back two weeks later and play FSU.

In 1991 – a year later – we were able to put aside winning the conference championship and start focusing on FSU. It helped, of course, that we were playing the Seminoles at home where, fortunately, we are now 12-0.

We're calling Ben Hill Griffin Stadium at Florida Field "The Swamp" now, because everyone knows nobody gets out of the swamp alive except the Gators.

9

OUR COACHING FAMILY

I f coaching staffs get along well together then the players will get along together. I've been on staffs where there were jealousies, some ego problems between offensive and defensive coaches. Once you have coaches who don't like each other, it transfers to the players. You'll soon have players not pulling for each other.

I'm a big believer that if we all pull together in the same direction we can achieve tremendous success. I decided long ago that I didn't know how many games we would win or lose, but we would have a coaching staff that got along with each other. No matter how talented an assistant coach might be, if he doesn't get along with the rest of the staff it will hurt your program.

We have a lot of social events during the year. For example, we take a family tubing party during the summer. Everybody – coaches, wives, staff, kids – gets on inner tubes and floats down the Ichetucknee River.

We also have "Gator Play Day" where we run about five miles in the morning, play tennis and other sporting events, and end up over at my house around the swimming pool talking about the events of the day.

In the spring of 1991 all the coaches and their wives went on a three-day cruise out of Cape Canaveral down to Nassau and back. The wives loved it because the coaches couldn't escape to a golf course, and we all had a great time just talking and cutting up.

We take all the coaches and their wives to the Key West Gator Club meeting and golf tournament each April, and the club members do a wonderful job of acting as hosts and hostesses. It's fun and helps build staff unity and togetherness.

Of course, everything we do as a staff is genuine, not forced. Our coaches are aware that attendance is not mandatory for them and their wives.

I tell our coaches that if we are having a little get-together during the off-season or after a game and they have friends they need to be with, they shouldn't feel obligated to come to my house or attend whatever function we are having. We want to keep it flexible, and I certainly understand that there are times when assistant coaches have family and friends visiting, and they need to be with them.

What we'll usually do after each home game is have a quick social time in the office, then split up and sometimes get together later. If there is something special to celebrate in addition to the game, we do it. When we played San Jose State in 1991 it was Norm Carlson's birthday, and the following week when we played Alabama it was the 25th wedding anniversary for Jerri and me, so we had cakes during our get-togethers after each of those games.

What we are trying to do is share a little camaraderie right after each game. Fortunately we haven't lost any home games at Florida yet, so there have been some very pleasant times. However, just like the players and coaches, our families are a close-knit group, and they win or lose together. When and if a home loss comes, we'll still get together and share the disappointment.

There isn't a bigger reason for the success we've enjoyed at Florida the past few years than my staff of assistant coaches.

When the team wins or I win an award, it is something that would have been impossible without these guys.

We have been fortunate – there have been only two changes among this group. Jim Bates, our defensive coordinator in 1990, got a superb opportunity with the Cleveland Browns and left in the spring of 1991. Inside linebacker coach Tim Marcum returned to the Arena Football League as head coach of the Detroit Drive and also joined Coach Mouse Davis as defensive coordinator of the New Jersey Knights of the World League. They were replaced on the defensive staff by Ron Zook and Charlie Strong, who both have made enormous contributions.

This was the staff that helped guide the Gators to the 1991 SEC championship:

RON ZOOK

Ron is an enthusiastic, energetic coach. He is like a lot of defensive secondary coaches who it often seems have hyper-type personalities. I don't think I've ever seen a coach who thoroughly enjoys coaching football any more than he does.

He is very demonstrative on the field, teaching his players in a way they understand. He is also the defensive coordinator, and he and the defensive staff are constantly meeting to try to come up with new ideas, finding whatever they can to help our players be successful.

Ron coached at several major universities, including Tennessee and Ohio State, and has worked under some outstanding head coaches. He told me he learned much of his philosophy from former Tennessee coordinator Ken Donahue, and has incorporated much of it at Florida.

Ron has a wonderful wife, Denise, and two daughters, Jacquelyn and Casey.

Denise, like most of the wives, isn't hesitant to speak up. I recall one day when we were all in Key West having a grand time. She turned around to Ron and said, "Ron, I love coming down here with the coaching staff. You had better coach your fanny off so we can return."

JIM COLLINS

Jim coaches the inside linebackers, but is so versatile he could coach almost any position and do it extremely well. He is well-organized and a sincere, soft-spoken person by nature, although he isn't at all bashful about speaking his mind when things aren't going right on the field.

He was at Duke University when I took the job there in 1987, having been on Steve Sloan's staff. I felt it was very important to keep him on my staff, and he has been with me since.

Jim is a good coach with an outstanding record as a recruiter. Most of the really tough recruiting jobs at Duke were done by Jim and two or three other coaches.

Geri, his wife, is our team photographer. She is on the sidelines at all of our games and has many memorable pictures from the past six years. She is always present with a camera at staff outings as well as games.

They have one daughter, Jennifer, who I think wants to be a cheerleader.

BOB SANDERS

Bob coaches the outside linebackers, runs our football camp and is just an excellent recruiter who works as hard as any coach I've ever been around.

Bob was also on my staff at Duke and was on Pepper Rodgers' staff with me at Georgia Tech in 1979. He was a part-time assistant then, but you could see some of the qualities then that now are his strengths.

He is very organized, keeps statistics and facts at hand at all times, and can find little tendencies of our opponents that help our team prepare. He is also a master at the punt-blocking game, and comes up with ways to get that done.

While Coach Collins runs our spring high school coaches clinic, for which we had a record 350 coaches last April, Coach Sanders runs the summer camp for high school athletes, and helped produce a record attendance there last summer.

Bob can get fiery at times, but generally he is a low-key type of coach who is constantly thinking. He and his wife, Kathie, have two daughters – Lindsay and Sarah – and a little boy, Robert, who was born in November of 1991. He is the first child born among our staff since we've been at Florida.

JERRY "RED" ANDERSON

Jerry probably has the hottest temper on the staff. After he screams and yells he comes back down to earth quickly. You need one coach like that on a staff, a guy who can get up in front of the team and say some inspirational words that put them at a high emotional level.

He is probably our most inspirational pregame speaker before the big traditional games like Georgia, Auburn and FSU.

Jerry coaches the defensive tackles. I promoted him to assistant head coach after the 1990 season because I felt that he was a man the players really respect, and he shares in handling the discipline problems. He is a liaison with our Office of Student Life in making sure our players are attending class and tutoring sessions and abiding by all the rules.

He and I were teammates at Florida for four years. He was the defensive captain of the 1966 team, so we had a lot of good times and heartaches together as players.

Jerry probably understands Florida history a little bit better than I do because he has coached here longer than I have. This alone makes him valuable.

I moved him from coaching the tight ends and special teams, which he did in 1989, to coaching defensive tackles because I thought that's really the area where his fire and emotion can show through to his players.

Coach Anderson deserves a lot of credit for teaching the techniques and fundamentals to his players and for the emotion with which they play. In 1991, both of his tackles, Brad Culpepper and Tony McCoy, were first team All-SEC, and Culpepper was an All-American.

Jerry and his wife, Mary Jean, have a grown son, Richard, and a daughter, Jennifer.

CHARLIE STRONG

Charlie coaches the defensive ends and blends in perfectly with our staff. He has an even disposition and never seems to get too high or too low, no matter what the situation.

He was on the Florida staff in 1989; and although I was impressed with him, I was not able to keep him at that point. I already had some defensive coaches to bring with me – Jim Bates and Tim Marcum – and had no other openings.

It impressed me that when I told Charlie he would not be kept on the 1990 staff, he said he understood and to keep him in mind if we had an opening someday because he would like to work for me and the University of Florida. When an opening came, I checked a little bit more with Coach Anderson, who was on the 1989 staff with Charlie, and with several other people around here and found out that I probably should have kept him the first year.

There are two things he doesn't have in common with the other coaches. He is a bachelor, and catches a lot of grief over that, and he doesn't play golf. He lays back and kids the other guys when they come in with a 95 or a 110.

CARL FRANKS

Carl has been with me as a player or coach most of the time since 1980, and probably knows me better than anybody on my staff. He is an important reason why I'm able to function as head coach, quarterback coach and offensive coordinator. He takes on many of the details without having to ask me what to do all the time.

Carl coaches the running backs and is our recruiting coordinator. He got into coaching in an unusual manner in 1984, while playing for me with the Tampa Bay Bandits of the USFL.

He had injured his knee during the 1983 season, and it just wasn't coming around. Meanwhile, one of our coaches – John Rauch – was moving into administration with the Bandits, and I had a chance to hire a running back coach.

Concerned about his injury, Carl came in one day to ask about what kind of disability income or salary would be available if his knee were not all right.

I said, "Let me ask you something. How would you like to coach the running backs here?"

Carl looked at me sort of funny and replied, "Are you serious?"

I had already made up my mind that he would be an excellent coach and told him the offer was serious: "You know all the drills, you know the offense, you know what we want done, you've been coached and you can coach them as well as anybody I can go find somewhere else."

He told me if I wanted him to coach them, he could coach them. He became a coach just like that. Carl went from player to coach in one day, and the Bandits didn't have to pay out any disability money, either.

His coaching career with the Bandits, with Duke and here at Florida all has been spent with running backs. He coached Gary Anderson at Tampa Bay, and a pair of collegiate 1,000-yard rushers: Randy Cuthbert of Duke in 1989 and Errict Rhett, who led the SEC in rushing for the Gators in 1991.

Before the 1991 season I appointed Carl recruiting coordinator because I believe one of the on-field coaches should have that title. Our first recruiting class was ranked number one in the nation by *SuperPrep Magazine,* so obviously Carl and the other coaches did an outstanding job.

Carl is married to a soft-spoken Southerner named Deborah. They have two daughters, Brittany and Courtney, who was born just before the 1992 season began.

RICH MCGEORGE

Rich is an excellent fundamentals coach of our offensive linemen. Though he is a low-key coach – not a screamer – when he needs to get on his players, he'll sure do it.

Rich is more into teaching techniques and encouraging his players. He is a players' coach who gets the most out of his people because they enjoy working with him.

He wanted to get into coaching in 1981, after 10 seasons as a tight end with the Green Bay Packers. He would commute to Durham from Winston-Salem, where he was living, to work with tight ends on a part-time basis at Duke. That's where I got to know him.

When the USFL started in 1983, Rich already had received a job offer from Rollie Dotsch to coach the tight ends and receivers for the Birmingham Stallions before I accepted the head coaching job at the Tampa Bay Bandits. He was in Birmingham for two years and joined me in Tampa in 1985 as offensive line coach.

When the USFL folded after that season, Rich was like the rest of us – he didn't coach anywhere in 1986. So he was eager and ready to come to Duke University with me in 1987, and we've been together since.

I think one of the best compliments that I have ever heard a line coach receive was from Coach Danny Ford of Clemson, who said that Rich's 1989 offensive line at Duke was the best pass-blocking line he had seen in the history of the ACC.

Rich and his wife, Bonnie, have two sons, both of whom are on football scholarships in the ACC. Randy is an offensive tackle at Duke, and Jason is a tight end at North Carolina State.

Many people ask me how I can be the head coach, quarterback coach and offensive coordinator at the same time. The biggest reason is that Rich and Carl Franks have been with me for so long that they know almost exactly what we want to do each week.

They get together and plan the protections each week, according to the other team's blitzes, and it really frees me up to basically look at the passing part of the total offensive scheme.

DWAYNE DIXON

Dwayne is a former great Gator wide receiver who now coaches our wide receivers. I think it is important for every staff to have two to four assistant coaches who are alumni of that school.

He played at Florida in the 1980s and was one of the gutsiest, most dependable receivers ever for the Gators. People still talk about some of the unbelievable catches he made. He would go down on the artificial turf and catch it or leap up in the air with defenders hanging on him – wherever the ball was he would go and get it.

He dropped only one pass in three years at Florida, and we don't believe in dropping them. Dwayne is a patient, confident coach who teaches fundamentals and techniques with a quiet, determined air that gives his receivers confidence.

Dwayne was working in our Office of Student Life, helping with the academic support system, when I got here in 1990. He and his wife, Sandra, were living in Yon Hall, the athletic dormitory.

He had played in the NFL with the Tampa Bay Bucs and bounced around the Arena League, where he was one of their star players. He then wound up back here at his alma mater.

I was able to bring him over to coach the wide receivers although he had never coached in his life. We just started him off as a full-time assistant coach. As quarterback coach, I meet with the players from both positions so I can help oversee the receivers.

It's not a position in which you need a veteran coach with years of experience. To me, it's a spot where if you have a chance to hire an alumnus of the school who fits in well with your staff, that is something you need to do.

Dwayne has been perfect for what we were looking for at that position. Ernie Mills led the conference in TD receptions the first year with 10, and in 1991 Willie Jackson led it in the same category, also with 10, trailed closely by our Harrison Houston and Tre Everett.

Dwayne and Sandra have a little girl, Brittany, and they were expecting another child as this book went to press. He is a great all-around athlete and a good man to have on your side in any athletic competition except possibly golf, although I hear he makes an occasional good shot in scramble tournaments.

JOHN REAVES

Most Gators know who John is from his days as a sophomore sensation in 1969, when Coach Ray Graves' last Florida team went 9-1-1 and beat SEC champion Tennessee in the Gator Bowl.

He was part of the "Super Soph" trio with Carlos Alvarez, the wide receiver, and Tommy Durrance, the running back.

That team really won the hearts of all Gator fans when, though not expected to do much, they became one of only seven Florida teams in history to win nine or more games in a season.

John broke many school, conference and NCAA records, some of which stand to this day. When Coach Graves retired and Doug Dickey replaced him, they still continued to throw the ball some, but did not quite have the success they had that first year.

John was a first-round NFL draft choice of the Philadelphia Eagles. He played for them and then bounced around the league. I had a chance to coach him with the Tampa Bay Bandits from 1983 to 1985.

A lot of people probably don't know it, but John threw for more than 4,000 yards in two straight seasons, 1984 and 1985. There have been only four quarterbacks in the history of pro football to have done that: Dan Marino, Dan Fouts, Jim Kelly and John Reaves.

When the league folded, John continued in his real-estate business in Tampa and later ran unsuccessfully for the state legislature. When I got the job at Florida, he called me and said he had a strong interest in coaching. I told him to make certain first that this was what he wanted to do with his life.

Coaching is something you really have to make a commitment to, as in "this is what I want to do with my life." You must make sure your wife and family understand what is involved and are completely supportive. John is fortunate to have a wonderful wife, Patti, and a solid family.

He met with them and called me back to say he wanted to coach at Florida in whatever position I could find for him. We appointed him tight end coach.

John also spends a lot of time with our young quarterbacks after practice, so he's our assistant quarterback coach as well. He does an outstanding job of making sure the quarterbacks are doing what they are supposed to in the off-season. That frees me up a lot from having to keep up with them every day.

John's first tight end – Kirk Kirkpatrick – led the SEC in receptions, and made first team all-conference and some of the All-America teams. He went on to play in the World League with Birmingham.

John is an outstanding recruiter. He works hard and his sincerity comes through when he talks to parents, prospects and high school coaches and administrators. He signed one of the best running backs in the state last year, Dwayne Mobley of Brooksville, Florida, and also the *USA Today* defensive player of the year, linebacker Dexter Daniels of Valdosta, Georgia.

He is a devoted Christian and actively involved in speaking at churches, high schools and youth groups. He just does a wonderful job in presenting a positive image of himself and the University of Florida.

He and Patti have three children, Layla, John David and Stephen.

We also have an administrative football assistant, Jamie Speronis, who works hard to keep all the details together for me and the entire staff; and an on-campus recruiting coordinator, Betty Ling, who does a super job. Betty handles mail-outs, travel arrangements for incoming prospects and the game-day procedures with prospects and their parents.

The chemistry is right with our staff, and all these various personalities blend together to make it work.

10

THE APPROACH
TO 1991

One of the most touching scenes I've ever experienced as a coach happened at our first practice in the spring of 1991. We were working out at night on Florida Field because many of the players had classes, tests or tutoring that afternoon, and we wanted the entire team at the opening practice.

I was standing near the 50-yard line while the kickers were working before practice. Tony McCoy came out in his football uniform for the first time since I'd come to Florida. He headed straight toward me.

Tony walked up with tears in his eyes and said, "Coach Spurrier, I just want to thank you for giving me another chance to get an education and play football. This is the greatest feeling I've ever had, being back here at Florida Field in a football uniform. The university won't regret this decision; I will make the most of this chance."

As most Gator fans know, Tony was suspended late in the 1989 season for an alleged sexual assault; however, all charges were later dropped when it was determined that he had been falsely accused. He was suspended from the university, went back home to Orlando, and got a job. Then he came to see me when I got the Florida job in January 1990.

He told me the details of what happened the night of the alleged assault. He was wearing a suit and tie, looked me right in the eyes and spoke with a sincere conviction that convinced me he was telling the truth. I firmly believe Tony is a good person who had been falsely accused. He told me he wanted to play football at Florida and graduate.

I sincerely felt Tony needed and deserved a second chance. I convinced athletic director Bill Arnsparger and dean of student affairs Jim Scott that Tony McCoy needed the University of Florida, and we needed Tony McCoy. He was allowed to re-enter school in 1990, but had to sit out the season. He had to go to summer school and pass about 17 hours to be eligible for the 1991 season. Tony is a good student. He did everything he was supposed to do academically and otherwise.

There's no doubt in my mind that we would not have achieved the goals set for 1991 without Tony. He was one of our best team leaders, a player all the other players looked up to with tremendous respect.

When we do our running drills after practice, we allow our players to take off their shoulder pads and helmets. Tony kept his on. If the team ran four laps, he ran five or six. When we run sprints, we try to get the players to finish hard all the way through the line. We never had to worry about him finishing.

Tony provided inspiration and leadership for the young guys. He was our leader in the locker room before games, at halftime and during the week. He was voted the most valuable player on the team by his teammates and given the "inspiration award" by the coaching staff. I strongly believe Tony will be a credit to our institution in the years to come as a graduate and a leader in his community.

I deeply appreciate and thank Jim Scott and everyone else involved in the decision to believe in Tony McCoy and give him a second chance.

Everyone connected with the team – coaches, players and

support staff – felt we had a chance to win the SEC championship again in 1991, this time officially.

We thought the other two best teams in the conference in 1991 were Alabama and Tennessee. Both of them were coming to Florida Field, where we hadn't lost a game in 1990 or even had one turn out close. We also had FSU coming to "The Swamp," as we call the field now.

Spring practice was excellent. I thought we really had a good chance with four starting offensive linemen returning – Tony Rowell, Cal Dixon, Mark White and Hesham Ismail – along with the starting defensive front of Harvey Thomas, Brad Culpepper, Tony McCoy and Mike Brandon.

Veteran defensive players Tim Paulk, Fee Bartley and Will White showed why they were all-conference performers. Then we got the bonus of freshman Larry Kennedy stepping in and playing all-star caliber football in his first college season.

Larry had not scored high enough on his college entrace exams coming out of high school in Sarasota in 1990. He signed with Ohio State, but never enrolled that year, choosing instead to work in Columbus, Ohio, and study for the SAT. During that fall he qualified with his SAT score and decided he didn't want to go to school at Ohio State, but wanted to come to Florida instead.

We had the nucleus – essentially the linemen – and the schedule was set up for us very nicely when Mississippi State decided to move their home game against us to Orlando from Starkville. That gave us five conference games in the state: three in Gainesville, one in Orlando and the annual game against Georgia in Jacksonville.

Our difficult road games were at LSU and Auburn, traditional powers who in 1991 struggled to 5-6 records.

I'm often accused of being too optimistic. So in the spring of 1991, when I went around the state to the Gator Clubs in different cities and spoke to the media, I always said we had a chance to win the SEC. I never claimed we were *going* to win it, just that we had a *chance*. However, I was thinking we had a *good* chance.

We had this good chance because of our team and the schedule, and because we still were hurting from the NCAA sanctions that kept us out of postseason play in 1990. We had won the 1990 title, but the SEC took it away and gave it to Tennessee because we were not eligible to go to the Sugar Bowl.

So there was a lot of animosity because we felt our 1990 players had been treated unfairly. The only way to do something about it was to take our frustration out on our opponents.

At the end of spring practice we elected Brad Culpepper, Tim Paulk and Cal Dixon as our captains, and we had the seniors set the goals for the coming season, something I had started at Duke in 1987.

I'm a big believer in goal-setting. I think you have to have long-term goals as well as short-term goals. We try to set our long-term goals at the end of spring practice, so that during the summer months our players can constantly be reminded of them.

We try to set goals that are attainable. I believe it is unrealistic – and you lose the purpose of goal-setting – if you set goals that you have virtually no chance of achieving.

I've still not had a team set a goal of winning the national championship, either because we just haven't felt we were quite at that point or because of the way the schedule fell that season. I hope that in the next three to four years we're going to have a team that says, with the way the schedule is set up and as good as we are, we believe we have a realistic chance to win it all this year.

I think that year is coming for the Gators.

In 1991, we had six goals:

1. We wanted to win the SEC again. We wanted to win it outright and be officially recognized as champions.

2. We wanted to win 10 games. No Florida team had ever won 10 games in a season, but we certainly felt this was attainable.

3. The players said: "We need to beat FSU. We haven't beaten them in four years. None of us has ever played in a victory over those guys." So beating FSU became a team goal.

4. We wanted to win the Sugar Bowl. We didn't just say we wanted to go to the Sugar Bowl – we wanted to win it. We felt if your goal is just to go to a bowl game you sort of lose focus on winning it. That, unfortunately, was a goal we didn't reach in 1991.

5. I think it was Brad Culpepper who said, "We think we have a chance to go undefeated." I told him that is extremely hard to do, but we'd put it among our goals. I told the seniors it would mean that if at some point during the season we were undefeated and I had to make a decision between attempting a two-point conversion to win a game or kicking the extra point to tie, I would choose the less-risky kick. Certainly if we were to finish undefeated we would have a shot at the national championship.

6. We wanted to finish the season ranked in the Top 10 in the nation.

We hit four of these six goals for the season, winning the SEC title, capturing 10 victories, defeating FSU and finishing in the Top 10. Perhaps one day we'll have a team that reaches all of its goals.

After our team meeting, with all the enthusiasm our players had, just about all of them wanted to stay around Gainesville during the summer session to get jobs and work out in preparation for the fall.

The local businessmen do an outstanding job of providing employment for our players. Summer employment in Gainesville for the players is excellent and totally legal. The players work hard for the money they earn, and the jobs are available for those who want to work.

You could sense the senior leadership emerging on this team, especially from the big linemen, guys such as Culpepper, McCoy, Rowell, White, Ismail and Dixon. Often the biggest, strongest, oldest guys have an opportunity to provide the most leadership. The younger guys will look up to them if they are doing everything they can and are busting their tails to improve and be as strong and quick as possible.

It was a good situation going into the 1991 season. I could sense these players were gearing up for the biggest year in

Florida history. That's why I felt so good about the chances of winning at least 10 games and all seven conference games. That would make this the best team in Gator history, and it was definitely a goal we had a chance to achieve.

We had a good preseason practice for the 1991 season. In our scrimmages, we had only one serious injury: Tight end Greg Keller broke his collarbone and was sidelined for the year. We had to suspend defensive end Darren Mickell for five games for violating athletic department policy; that hurt the team and him.

Darren is a great talent who had difficulty doing what was required of him in order to represent the Gators. I like him, and I hope he has learned from his experiences and will make choices that benefit him in the future. He has the ability to be a star in the NFL.

The season opened at home against San Jose State, a team that had gone 9-2-1 the previous year and had won the California Raisin Bowl. Terry Shea, their coach, felt like they had a fine team coming back, although they had lost a lot of seniors from the '90 team.

Coach Shea said that he was coming to Gainesville to win the game. He said San Jose State would not be intimidated playing the Gators at Florida Field because they could line up against just about any team in the nation.

His repeated remarks about how they could come to Florida and beat us on our own field certainly got the attention of our coaching staff and players. We generated quite a lot of emotion for that game, as we had for the opening game in my first season with the Gators.

It turned out to be a game in which we scored a lot of points quickly. In fact, it probably will be the only season I'll ever have in which we score on the very first offensive play of the year.

We kicked off, and on their second play they fumbled; Brad Culpepper scooped it up on their 23-yard line. On our first play we had a pass called, and they blitzed us – their defensive package was blitz-blitz-blitz – so Shane, who saw it coming, changed the play at the line with an audible and made a nice throw on a corner route to Harrison Houston for the touchdown.

Harrison hadn't known he would be starting for the first time in his career until after the warmups. Tre Everett, our outstanding starting wide receiver, had injured a hamstring early in the week, but he had felt he would be ready to go by Saturday. During the warmups we could tell Tre wasn't anywhere near being ready to go full speed, so I told Harrison he was going to start.

On our next series, on second-and-one, they blitzed again. Shane audibled to another corner route, Harrison ran another perfect route, there was another nice throw and we had another touchdown on our third play of the game. Harrison wound up catching three TD passes in his debut as a starter.

We had the most points I can ever remember a team of mine having at halftime in a game. We went up and down the field, the defense got us some turnovers, and there were 45 points on the scoreboard at halftime.

It's hard to yell at your guys in the locker room at halftime when you've just scored 45 points. So we told them that the starters would play only one series in the third quarter, and then we'd give the backups a chance to play. I told them we expected them to do the same thing, go up and down the field and score touchdowns.

Shane and the starters took the ball straight in for a touchdown on their only possession to make it 52-14, and then the subs took over, managing one more score. We had 59 points with more than 20 minutes left in the game. From that point on we sputtered. Our second-team offensive line didn't block very well, our second and third unit backs didn't do very much, and it got really sloppy the rest of the way.

San Jose State threw for more than 350 yards against us, which was disturbing to a lot of people and especially disturbing to our defensive coaches. Ron Zook, our defensive coordinator and secondary coach, made some changes after that game. We found out that freshman Larry Kennedy needed to be starting at cornerback, and he proved to be a very valuable player for us later on.

San Jose State had a chance to score more than their 21 points, but fumbled inside our two-yard line and made other mistakes. It was a solid opening win, but it had fans and the media talking the next week about how porous our secondary was, and what a team like FSU would do to us.

I take each game on its own merits. You can't assume or project that what happens one week will happen the next, and you certainly can't look 10 weeks down the schedule, because teams change as the season rolls along.

Overall, we were happy with the results of the first game of the 1991 season. Immediately afterwards, though, we started thinking about Alabama, our next opponent.

ROAD TO THE CHAMPIONSHIP

GAME ONE

Florida 59, San Jose State 21
September 7, 1991, Ben Hill Griffin Stadium

GAINESVILLE, FLA. – The largest crowd in the history of football in the state of Florida, 83,067, watched Florida open its 1991 season with a solid 59-21 victory over San Jose State.

Gator quarterback Shane Matthews threw five touchdown passes, tying an SEC record, connecting three times with wide receiver Harrison Houston, who was making his first career start.

Following a fumble recovery on the Spartan 22-yard line by tackle Brad Culpepper, Florida scored on its first offensive play of the season when Matthews teamed with Houston on a touchdown pass.

Less than three minutes later, UF made it 14-0 when Matthews and Houston combined on a 46-yard pass play. Matthews, 17 of 22 for 272 yards for the day, was named SEC Player of the Week for his performance.

San Jose State fought back with quarterback Matt Veatch directing a drive of 72 yards, which led to a 44-yard TD pass to Bryce Burnett. Following a 30-yard field goal by Florida's Arden

FLORIDA 59, SAN JOSE STATE 21

TEAM STATISTICS

	SJSU	UF
First Downs	19	22
Rushes-Yards	33-83	33-127
Passing Yards	388	339
Passes	23-46-1	21-31-2
Total Offense	471	466
Penalties/Yards	13-94	9-98
Fumbles-Lost	5-3	2-1
Possession Time	32:20	27:40

| San Jose State | 7 | 7 | 7 | 0 | – | 21 |
| Florida | 17 | 28 | 14 | 0 | – | 59 |

INDIVIDUAL LEADERS

Rushing: SJSU – Hawthorne 6-30 1TD, Ellerbe 8-23; Florida – Rhett 12-75, McClendon 7-30 1TD, Ackerman 3-10, Dean 3-8, Robinson 1-7, Bilkie 1-4, Ferdinand 1-4.

Passing: SJSU – Veatch 23-41-388-1 Int, 2TD; Florida – Matthews 17-22-272-1 Int, 5TD, Fox 3-6-67 1TD, Dean 3-1-0-1 Int

Receiving: SJSU – Burnett 3-88 2TD, Lindsey 4-65; Florida – Rhett 6-92, Houston 4-78 3TD, Sullivan 3-40, W. Jackson 2-31 1TD, McClendon 2-26 1TD, Hill 1-54, McNabb 1-12, Rushing 1-6

Czyzewski, the Spartans scored on a short plunge of one yard to cut the Gators' lead to 17-14 early in the second quarter.

Florida quickly put the game out of reach with a 28-point explosion to make the score 45-14 at halftime. Houston started the barrage with a 14-yard TD pass from Matthews with 8:13 left in the half. On San Jose State's next possession Gator linebacker

Carlton Miles picked off a Veatch pass attempt and took it 10 yards for a TD to make it 31-14. Willie Jackson's first collegiate TD, a 24-yard pass from Matthews, was followed by a two-yard scoring run by Willie McClendon with 22 seconds left in the half.

In the third quarter Matthews' 17-yard touchdown pass to McClendon on Florida's first possession ended the junior signal-caller's activity for the afternoon. Reserves came on and quarter-back Brian Fox completed the Gators' scoring with a 54-yard TD toss to Aubrey Hill. ■

11

BEATING
A RESPECTED TEAM

Our game against Alabama was the first SEC game in the completed, expanded Ben Hill Griffin Stadium at Florida Field. We added about 10,000 seats in the north end zone and put in 18 skyboxes called "Gator Dens," plus a lounge area called the "Touchdown Terrace."

Jeremy Foley, who was senior associate athletic director at the time and has since been promoted to athletic director, coordinated this vast project for the athletic department. It completed what I believe is one of the best football stadiums in the country.

This stadium doesn't have a track around the field; it was built solely for football, and our fans are closer to the action than at just about any stadium I have ever seen. Coincidentally, Alabama was the opponent in the dedication game for the original Florida Field in 1930. We certainly didn't want to repeat history; Alabama won 20-0 back then.

I have a great deal of respect for the University of Alabama, its football program and its fans. Over the years Bama has been the premier team of the SEC, and their players and fans know how to win or lose with class.

The opportunity to compete against this program meant a lot to me and to our team, and we looked forward to a healthy confrontation in which controversy would play no part.

Unfortunately, actions by some members of the media in Birmingham turned it into one of the most emotional weeks I've had as a coach heading into an important game. It was depressing and disgusting, and it didn't need to happen.

In this business, rumors and misquotes happen all the time, and all you can do is try to be honest and straightforward and not let it bother you. That is easier said than done, and the situation before the Alabama game is one I'll never forget.

About the last week of August, our on-campus recruiting coordinator, Betty Ling, told me a Gator fan living in Birmingham, Alabama, had called to tell her there was something being spread up there about me predicting a 30-point victory for the Gators over Alabama. He said they were saying on sports call-in shows that a story in the *Atlanta Journal-Constitution* reported I had made this prediction at a Gator Club meeting in the off-season.

I should have called Tony Barnhart at the *Journal* to check this out. He is an objective, honest reporter who would have set me straight on what happened, on what was written or not written.

I didn't think to do that, however, and I just assumed something false had been written there in Atlanta.

I wrote Alabama coach Gene Stallings immediately so he would understand, in case he read the story, that it simply wasn't true. Coach Stallings wrote me back and said he understood and looked forward to seeing me when the game came up.

It turned out there never was anything in the newspaper about that. The rumor started, according to radio talk show host Doug Layton in Birmingham, when a man called his talk show and said he had read this in the Atlanta papers.

Radio talk shows give a forum to this type of rumor-mongering, and I think they should be considered as entertainment, not journalism. This report should have ended that day on Layton's show.

However, the week of the game it was pursued by sportswriter Charles Hollis of the *Birmingham News*. Before he was through he made it appear that the original report was factual.

The way the story went, I was supposed to have made this bold prediction at a Gator Club meeting in Tallahassee in August. Actually, there wasn't such a meeting in August; that particular club meeting had been back in April.

During the past few years, Hollis has been very critical of the University of Florida. It seems he has a strong dislike of the Gators, and since I've become the coach at Florida he's passed that dislike on to me.

Hollis had strongly insinuated in an article the week of our Kentucky game in 1990 that our players and coaches, including me, were cheaters who didn't deserve to finish first in the conference, and that it would be a good thing for the league if the Wildcats beat us. Never mind that no coaches or players at Florida were even around for the one alleged violation in 1986.

After Hollis magnified the false talk-show chatter, I started getting calls from the media. I denied the rumor, of course, because I never said we would beat Alabama by 30 points, or by any margin, as a matter of fact. Can you imagine a rational coach making any sort of prediction like that?

Perhaps this rumor started from a talk I gave after the Orange and Blue Game to the Golden Gators – a group of UF supporters 70 years old or older. Many of them had been there that day in 1930 when Florida and Alabama dedicated Florida Field.

I told them we wanted to dedicate the Alabama game to the Golden Gators. Alabama, the SEC's premier team since its inception in 1933, has won more conference championships than any other team, probably twice as many as the next closest team. When you talk about SEC football, the number one team is Alabama, without a doubt.

I added that if the University of Florida ever wants to be considered one of the very best in our conference, we need to beat
Alabama. In the history of our school we had never beaten them
in Florida, so this was a chance to make history.

The additional 10,000 fans in our stadium, thanks to the expan-
sion, gave us a big advantage playing Alabama in Gainesville. It
meant we might be able to defeat them there, and if we could, I
wanted the Golden Gators to know the game was dedicated to
them. I joked that if we could beat them by the largest margin in
history, it wouldn't have to be by much, since all of our wins up in
Alabama had been close.

However, there wasn't any prediction of a 30-point win. There
wasn't even a prediction of a win, just hopeful thinking that
maybe we could do it in our stadium.

The false reports out of Birmingham made it a very trying
week for me. I didn't want to comment further and drag it on,
but questions from the media on this subject came my way
every day. I'm not one to say "no comment" whether I'm right or
wrong, but especially if I'm right.

If we were to lose the game, if this created controversy that
would help cost us the game, it was obvious that many writers
would say that Spurrier's big mouth cost the Gators. I got as
emotionally ready to coach this game as any I've ever had. The
fear of losing was so great.

During the week, one of the Alabama players said, "I wish
Spurrier were playing in the game." That really hurt me, because
as coaches we don't need to have words with opposing players. I
don't believe coaches should have any confrontations with players on the other team, and this was probably even truer that
week because of my respect for the Alabama program.

I tried to excuse what he said, because he didn't understand
that this situation had been instigated by false reports and glori-
fied by a newspaper reporter with an ax to grind.

Fortunately, my players really backed me up on this deal. I
think some of the comments the Alabama guys made about me

Coach Ray Graves was the leading force behind the Gators in the 1960s. It was under Graves' tutelage that Steve Spurrier won the Heisman Trophy in 1966. Graves, the winningest coach in Gator history (70-31-4), led Florida to five bowl games, winning four.

Newlyweds Steve and Jerri Spurrier enjoy a relaxing day in the fall of 1966.

This photo of Spurrier graced many magazine covers in 1966.

Florida assistant head coach Gene Ellenson (left) and head coach Ray Graves look on during action in the 1960s.

Coaching staff of the 1991 SEC Champion Gators: (from left) John Reaves, Dwayne Dixon, Ron Zook, Bob Sanders, Jerry Anderson, Steve Spurrier, Charlie Strong, Jim Collins, Carl Franks and Rich McGeorge.

Florida captured its first official SEC Football Championship Trophy in 1991 after posting a 7-0 conference record. It was the first time since 1977 that an SEC team won seven conference games in a season.

Steve Spurrier and the Gators pose for pictures at the Superdome in New Orleans before the '92 Sugar Bowl.

Coach Spurrier looks on as the Gators defensive unit goes to work.

Jerri Spurrier and daughter Amy enjoy the festivities before the 1991 Florida-Georgia game. Amy and her sister Lisa (not pictured) both are graduates of the University of Florida.

Florida coaches and their wives got away in the spring of 1991 on a three-day cruise from Cape Canaveral to Nassau in the Bahamas and back. The wives especially enjoyed themselves because the coaches couldn't sneak off to play golf.

Coach Spurrier and faculty representative Dr. Nick Cassisi celebrate win over Kentucky at a gathering at the Spurriers' home.

A relaxing moment for Jerri Spurrier at a meeting of the Key West Gator Club.

University of Florida President Dr. John Lombardi congratulates Coach Spurrier after the Gators beat Kentucky 47-15 to finish first in the SEC in 1990.

In 1990 the Gators defeated the host Kentucky Wildcats to finish first in the SEC – but they were not awarded the official title because of NCAA sanctions.

Running back Errict Rhett celebrates after scoring on a third-and-two sweep to clinch the victory over Kentucky in 1991.

The Gators proved they deserved to win the SEC championship and the Sugar Bowl bid with their 35-26 victory over a determined Kentucky team. A photo session after the game captures the euphoria that could be felt throughout Ben Hill Griffin Stadium.

The game against Alabama on September 14, 1991, was the first SEC game played in the newly expanded Ben Hill Griffin Stadium. Approximately 10,000 seats were added in the north end zone. In addition, 18 skyboxes called Gator Dens and a lounge area, Touchdown Terrace, were constructed. The Gators went on to trounce Alabama in that game, 35-0.

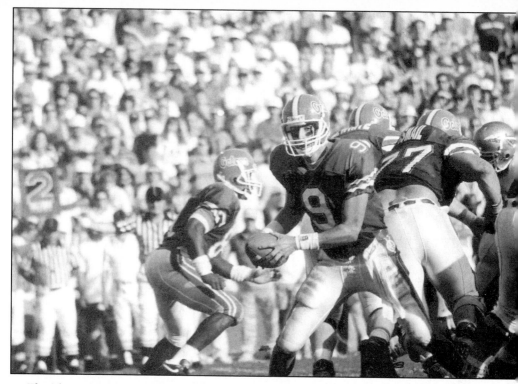

Florida quarterback Shane Matthews propelled his Gators to a hard-fought 14-9 victory over third-ranked Florida State in 1991. Matthews completed 13 of 30 passes for 208 yards and one touchdown.

Coach Spurrier gives his team the once-over during pregame warmups.

A disgusted Steve Spurrier looks on as Notre Dame rallies from a nine-point deficit to defeat the injury-riddled Gators 39-28 in the 1992 Sugar Bowl. It was the Gators' first trip to the Sugar Bowl since 1974.

Florida cheerleaders lead the team onto the Florida Citrus Bowl field in Orlando for the Texaco Star Classic against Mississippi State. Errict Rhett rushed for 142 yards as the Gators triumphed and upped their conference record to 2-0 in September 1991.

Coach Spurrier
paces the sideline
while defensive
coordinator Ron
Zook (center) and
linebackers coach
Jim Collins focus on
the action.

ESPN's Adrian Karsten interviews Coach Spurrier after the Gators ran their SEC
record to 4-0 with a 35-18 victory over fourth-ranked Tennessee. The Gators'
victory avenged a 45-3 drubbing by the Vols in 1990.

Ron Zook (left), Spurrier and former Gator assistant head coach Gene Ellenson toast the Gators' 1991 SEC title at a gathering at Spurrier's house following the victory over Kentucky.

Assistant coach Rich McGeorge (left), Spurrier and assistant coach Jim Collins review the events of the day at a postgame get-together at the Spurriers' home.

There were those who doubted that Shane Matthews could really play quarterback at Florida, but he has proven them all wrong. Matthews came on strong and led the Gators to a first-place conference finish in 1990 and to the SEC Championship in 1991, earning the SEC Player of the Year honor both years.

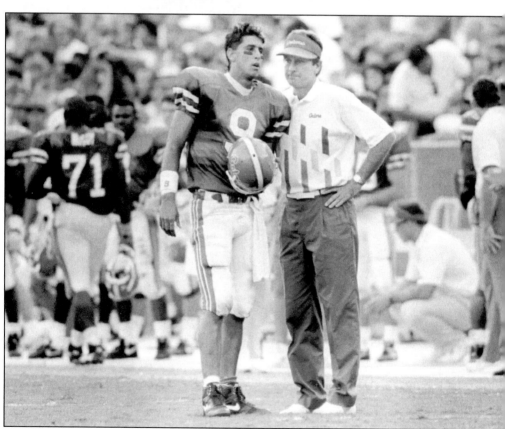

Coach Spurrier and Shane Matthews talk strategy. Spurrier: "Some people have trouble accepting criticism from their coaches, but not Shane, it just bounces off him. ... I don't believe you could ask for a higher-quality person to work with ..."

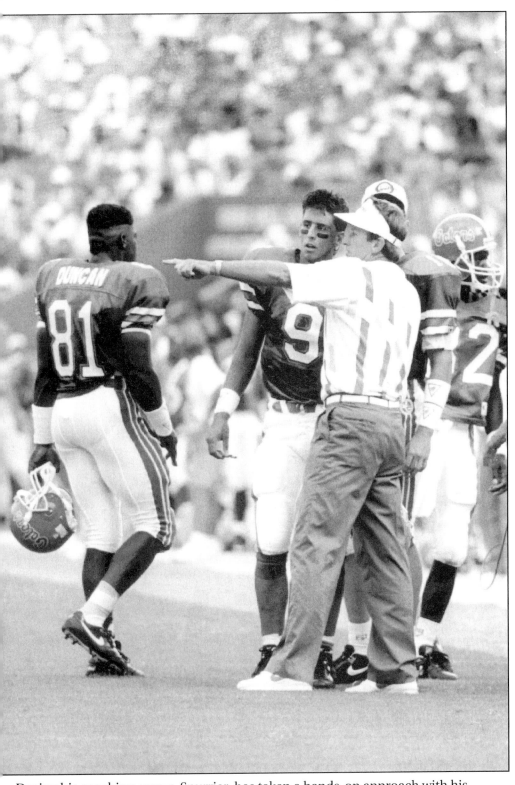

During his coaching career, Spurrier has taken a hands-on approach with his offensive players. At Florida, he quickly rejuvenated a struggling Gator offense and produced the most explosive attack in the Southeastern Conference.

Spurrier on coach Ron Zook (kneeling): "Ron is a very enthusiastic, energetic coach. ... I don't think I've ever seen a coach who thoroughly enjoys coaching football any more than he does."

Florida's seniors capped their college careers by leading the Gators to the 1992 Sugar Bowl at the Louisana Superdome in New Orleans, where they got together before the game to savor the moment.

inspired our players, who were determined that they were not going to make their coach look bad.

Finally, the game arrived. Our fans were as loud as they have been in the history of Florida Field, and the place was jammed. In pregame warmups the noise was deafening, on a perfect night for football.

I looked around and thought: "This is why I'm here. This level of competition is why you coach."

We played very sporadically on offense the entire first half. Alabama's outstanding defense did the job, and we just couldn't seem to make even a first down; things were going bad and it was frustrating.

Our defense was playing outstanding ball to keep us in the game. Some of the individual plays were remarkable. I remember Brad Culpepper making a tackle on fourth-and-one when our defense was really out of position. He tackled Siran Stacey for a two-yard loss when Stacey might have gone all the way because of our poor alignment.

We did make a little drive right before the half that resulted in a field goal, which seemed to swing the entire momentum of the game in our direction.

We got the ball with 38 seconds left, and Alabama played their five-short, three-deep defense as they normally do in this situation. Their inside linebackers really jumped our short men, covering them tightly, so we decided to go to medium-length passes.

We were able to hit Alonzo Sullivan on two 17- or 18-yard crossing patterns, to get big chunks of yards and stop the clock. It was also the first time that season we used our no-back offense. We split five receivers and really stretched the field in order to find some seams in the defense.

On the last play of the half, the horn went off as Arden Czyzewski's 48-yard field goal attempt sailed through the air on the way to giving us a 6-0 lead. The crowd exploded and the pandemonium carried our team into the locker room. It seemed as though this had loosened the dam, as if the momentum of the game had turned on that kick.

You could feel it at halftime with our team. We really were pumped up waiting for the second half to start, and the pressure of the first half seemed to be lifted off the players' shoulders. We were ready to go out relaxed, get after Alabama and play with confidence.

It was a good feeling.

Early in the third quarter we blitzed on one play, and Will White had the tight end in man-to-man coverage. The throw came in a little behind the receiver, and Will made a beautifully timed interception.

That set us up on their 34-yard line, and Dexter McNabb ran for 11 yards on a draw on first down. Then Shane Matthews came through with the sort of play that makes him such a winner.

Alabama blitzed us on first down, and Shane hit Tre Everett on a corner route for the game's first touchdown. The protection was decent at best, not great, but it was an outstanding throw right on the money by Shane. As he let it go about three guys hit him – high, low and in between – and Shane made a gutsy, beautiful throw even though he knew he would be clobbered and never see it completed.

He shook off the hit and hit Sullivan over the middle on a two-point conversion after the touchdown, and we had a 14-0 lead. This margin gave us a chance to mix it up with more effective use of our running game.

The running of Errict Rhett really opened up the game in the second half. We had put in a little cut-back play: The quarterback tosses it back as if it's a one-back sweep going wide right. When the running back catches it, he takes about two steps and then cuts back the other way.

Alabama's defense was flowing all night. Our running game was getting stuffed, but this little counter, cut-back play really hurt their defense and put them off balance. Of Errict's 170 yards rushing, more than 100 came on this play alone.

The combination of our running game and our defense gave us control of the game. The defense just crushed the Alabama offense as Tony McCoy and Brad Culpepper probably had their best game ever as a tandem.

Meanwhile, Willie Jackson was catching everything in sight. His first TD reception put us ahead 21-0. He then came back to catch a ball from Shane on about the five-yard line, turn it upfield and just run over the defensive back and dive into the end zone. It was one of the finest plays of the year by a player who just had the desire to get into the end zone.

We had our second-team players in during most of the fourth quarter, and managed to run one in to make the final score 35-0. Standing there relaxed on the sideline, I couldn't help but think about that falsely reported prediction of a 30-point victory, but we would have tried to score that final time whether that story was written or not.

When we put backup players in the game we certainly aren't going to tell them not to play hard and try to score. We won't call time out to run up the score, but you had better believe we are going to run our offense and attempt to put points on the board.

That night was a very special time for the group of Golden Gators that I had promised to dedicate the game to in the spring. They have followed the Gators longer than anyone, and it was wonderful that this could happen for them.

I don't remember ever being so drained after a game. The magnitude of the competition combined with the terribly trying time caused by the false reports out of Birmingham had taken a toll.

Our 25th wedding anniversary was the day of the game, and friends had a cake for Jerri and me that night. I was almost too tired to eat any and certainly made little conversation about what should have been one of the happiest moments in my coaching career.

I just hope that kind of false story never pops up again.

ROAD TO THE CHAMPIONSHIP

GAME TWO

Florida 35, Alabama 0
September 14, 1991, Ben Hill Griffin Stadium

GAINESVILLE, FLA. – Sixth-ranked Florida broke open a tight game in the second half and went on to pummel Alabama 35-0 before a record crowd of 85,069.

It was the first victory ever for a Florida team over Alabama in the state, and it was the worst shutout loss for the Crimson Tide since 1977.

Florida's defense kept the game under control for the Gators in the first half as the offense sputtered. Alabama penetrated into Florida territory three times and came away scoreless, while the Gators scored on 44-yard and 48-yard field goals by Arden Czyzewski.

It was Czyzewski's 48-yarder as the first half ended that appeared to set the tone for the second-half surge by Florida, which scored 29 points after intermission.

Will White's interception in the third quarter gave the Gators excellent field position at the Alabama 34-yard line, and they scored in two plays.

Dexter McNabb gained 11 on a draw play, then quarterback Shane Matthews lofted a perfect 23-yard strike to streaking Tre Everett in the end zone for the first TD of the game. Matthews, who appeared shaken by a hit as he was throwing, came back to toss a two-point conversion to Alonzo Sullivan to make it 14-0.

The next Florida touchdown capped a drive highlighted by the running of tailback Errict Rhett, who carried four times for 52 yards in a series to set up a 15-yard TD pass from Matthews to Willie Jackson, upping the margin to 21-0.

Matthews added a five-yard touchdown pass to Jackson, and Rhett finished off the final drive of the evening with a three-yard scoring run to bring it to 35-0.

FLORIDA 35, ALABAMA 0

TEAM STATISTICS

	UA	UF
First Downs	15	23
Rushes-Yards	45-140	39-216
Passing Yards	117	251
Passes	9-20-2	15-27-2
Total Offense	257	467
Penalties/Yards	9-84	6-34
Fumbles-Lost	6-3	2-1
Possession Time	30:22	29:38

| Alabama | 0 | 0 | 0 | 0 | – | 0 |
| Florida | 0 | 6 | 15 | 14 | – | 35 |

INDIVIDUAL LEADERS

Rushing: Alabama – Stacy 17-80, Lassic 5-22, Turner 5-20; Florida – Rhett 23-170 1TD, McNabb 6-34, McClendon 5-27

Passing: Alabama – Barker 4-11-62 2 Int, Woodson 4-8-50; Florida – Matthews 15-27-251 2 Int, 3TD

Receiving: Alabama – Wimbley 3-34, Finley 2-25; Florida – Everett 5-97 1TD, Houston 4-91, W. Jackson 2-25 2TD, T. Jackson 2-11, Sullivan 1-14, McClendon 1-13

Matthews threw for 251 yards and three touchdowns, while Rhett carried the ball 23 times for 170 yards and one score. The Gator defense held Alabama to 257 yards of total offense.

For Florida, defensive tackle Brad Culpepper's outstanding performance earned him the SEC Defensive Player of the Week award.

The victory moved the Gators to 2-0 and the 16th-ranked Crimson Tide fell to 1-1. ∎

12

SYRACUSE SLUMBER

Following the emotional week of the Alabama game I came up with a new game plan for myself. Unfortunately, it turned out that it didn't work for me.

Some friends told me, and a couple of people even wrote in to say, that they were concerned my zealous, emotional approach on Saturdays might lead to early burnout. One letter said, "Coach, the way you are so emotional on the sideline, the way you get so involved in cheering them on – how long do you think you can do this? You might get burned out as a coach real early!"

I thought about that, about the frustration of seeking perfection on every play and my eagerness to seek the effort, concentration and execution I know our players can achieve. It does result in me slamming my visor to the turf from time to time. It is not so much in anger at a player as it is in my utter disappointment in our failure to accomplish what I believe could be accomplished at that moment.

After hearing these concerns and reflecting on my normal game-day demeanor, I decided to make a change the week of the Syracuse game. I thought, this week I'll act like most head coaches.

I'll be calm, cool and collected. In practice I won't scream and holler too much. Since the game is indoors, I won't even wear a visor.

I will try to act like a coach who plans to be here for 20 years; I'll pace myself and not get so emotionally involved in the game.

Our team was coming off that big win over Alabama, and they faced another talented SEC team, Mississippi State, the week after the Syracuse game. Syracuse hadn't looked very good on tape in its win over Maryland the previous week.

As it turned out, our team needed their head coach to be emotional and to drive them. My decision to do the opposite that week was a mistake. We had no idea Coach Paul Pasqualoni and his team would be laying for us the way they were. It turned out they had an excellent game plan on offense, which kept us off-balance all afternoon. Their defense played the way they always did, but they outhit us from start to finish.

All week long Coach Pasqualoni had done his best Vince Dooley imitation. At one point he even said Florida had seven or eight future first-round NFL draft choices. Our players soaked up all this praise; we were a very complacent, overconfident team on our trip to Syracuse.

The domed stadium and artificial turf, in my opinion, played no part in our loss. Syracuse would have beaten us that day outdoors on grass. I had heard that the Carrier Dome noise level was tremendous, but the crowd noise is much, much louder at Florida Field, Neyland Stadium and the Gator Bowl than it was there that day. We were able to hear our signals easily all day.

At the Friday night meal I could sense we were not ready to play. Sometimes in coaching you will get fooled about the mental state of your team for a particular contest. There have been times I've thought my team was fired up and they weren't, and other times when I've worried needlessly that they would be flat. This time I was absolutely certain the Gators did not have enough concern about or respect for Syracuse.

I told our team we were big favorites and Syracuse had nothing to lose. I said, "To beat us Syracuse has to try some things like a reverse on a kickoff. Let's look for reverses, let's look for throwback passes. You've got to look for anything and everything when you are a big favorite."

In the locker room right before the game, even Tony McCoy, our outstanding defensive tackle, was quiet. He is normally an outgoing, get-after-them motivator for the team.

Just before we went out for the TV introductions – ABC was broadcasting the game – I told the kickoff coverage team to look for a reverse on the opening kickoff. It fell on deaf ears. After we watched Kirby DarDar run right past our bench on the way to a 95-yard touchdown on a reverse on the opening kickoff, I asked three members of the coverage team if they had heard me talk about watching for that play. All of them said no. Then Arden Czyzewski, who kicked off on the play, came up and said, "He only mentioned it three or four times right before it happened."

I could tell we were not concentrating. We have a little routine right before we go out onto the field, in which we gather around and I yell, "Who is going to play for 60 minutes?" The team responds, "Gators, Gators, Gators!" Then we go out and try to do just that.

At Syracuse I had called them all up and told them to put their hands in the circle for our routine. All of a sudden, defensive end Mike Brandon jumped in ahead of me and shouted, "Who's going to kick ass?" Everybody shouted, "Gators, Gators, Gators!" and ran out on the field.

Mike probably had thought we weren't primed and needed some prodding. I wasn't happy. We hadn't done it that way before; but I thought, I'm not going to get mad at him today. I'm going to be calm, cool and collected.

That opening reverse by Syracuse was a combination of excellent execution and very poor coverage, and it set the tone for the day. Syracuse fielded it deep and the player who received it started right, then handed the ball to DarDar, who came back left, turned it upfield and streaked down the sideline for the score. We were 14 seconds into the game.

We had an offensive game plan set up in which I was going to signal in the plays and let the offensive linemen watch me, in case the noise was too bad for them to hear Shane Matthews repeat the calls. We figured all Shane would have to do is go up to the line of scrimmage and say, "hut-hut," and away we'd go. We did that for three plays in the first possession and went nowhere – it was no gain, penalty and quarterback sack.

On our second possession we had three more plays, went nowhere again and got another penalty, which is a good sign of lack of concentration.

This time Syracuse swirled right down the field for another TD. The game was three or four minutes old, and we were down 14-0. You could tell on the field that the Syracuse team was gaining confidence and momentum. Looking across the field and watching their excited conversation, hand-slapping and urging on of teammates, I knew that the emotion on their bench was much higher all day than it was on ours.

Syracuse had entered the game hoping they might beat us. Then these good things happened, and you could feel they were becoming confident. They were beginning to think, hey, we can beat these guys, they're not that tough.

We were behind the entire game. We got within seven points one time; but every time we threatened to get back into the game, here they came with the option play, the pass off of it or the sprint draw.

We were back on our heels on defense. If we set up for a pass, they ran the option. If we expected option, they ran the sprint draw. If we expected sprint draw, they passed. It was that sort of day against an offensive game plan that was masterfully drawn up and executed perfectly.

Offensively, we were out of sync most of the day. It was a dropped pass here, a bad throw there, a missed blocking assignment, a penalty and, generally, the lack of a running game. We lost 17 yards rushing for the day, and you won't beat many teams doing that.

It was a game we didn't deserve to win, and we lost 38-21.

When we got back to Gainesville and watched the offensive

and defensive tapes of the game, we discovered we'd had only one hard hit in 60 minutes of football. Myrick Anderson hit their tailback in the backfield and created a fumble that we recovered at their seven-yard line. It led to a touchdown.

In contrast, the Syracuse players hit us with all they had all day. Their defensive backs, in particular, were reckless and aggressive. I recall a fourth-and-14 pass play where Shane hit receiver Harrison Houston right in the numbers, but Syracuse's defensive back gave it all he had and hit Harrison with a solid shot just as the ball got there to knock it away.

That was a typical play for Syracuse that day. We were out-coached, outhit and soundly whipped. It was a good tail-kicking, and how we would respond would determine the future of our 1991 season.

The silence on the flight home gave me some hope that we were at least thinking about what had happened. I didn't know how that would be converted into action and results.

After we viewed the tapes on Sunday while our players were taking the off-day required by NCAA rules, I told our coaches we were going to run the stadium steps at dawn on Tuesday.

The first contact we coaches have with players after a Saturday game is on the following Monday at a four o'clock team meeting. We don't practice until Monday night, giving players all day to catch up on classwork and tutoring, and to get in some weightlifting. At the meeting I said, "Fellas, we're going to meet here at 6:30 in the morning to run the stadium steps."

Just the thought of how we all had been stinking up the place at Syracuse made me boil. I added, "If anybody doesn't like it they can quit the team; they can leave, it doesn't matter to me. We're not going to play with the same effort we played with at Syracuse. You guys that played hard should appreciate us doing this. You guys that didn't play very hard, if you want to leave the team because you don't want to get up that early in the morning, that's fine."

All of the guys understood. They felt we needed to do this; we had to do something because we could not allow them to represent the University of Florida with the effort level demonstrated at Syracuse.

We – coaches and players – had our good little run up and down the stadium steps at 6:30 that morning. Nobody complained too much. That was the only time we ran the stadium steps in '91, but it was a good reminder that we're not going to put up with an effort that is not our best.

As coaches, we can take losing as long as we've played as hard and as smart as we can. When we don't make our best effort, the team is going to get a strong reminder that this is not acceptable. And, yes, I vowed never again to be a calm, cool and collected head coach. That's just not me, so maybe Tim Sain and Bud Fernandez, our equipment men, had better keep a large supply of visors handy.

The loss at Syracuse did help us. Obviously, without great effort we were an ordinary team, and that game proved this fact to our players. We were heading back into SEC play against Mississippi State, and we were off and running in the league with a 1-0 conference record, after having beaten a very good Alabama team.

As our captains stressed to the team after the Alabama game: We'd had a good win, but every conference game counted the same in the standings, and anything less than our top effort wouldn't be enough the rest of the way.

Except for lapses in portions of the Northern Illinois and Kentucky games, games we were fortunate enough to win anyway, we played at maximum effort the rest of the season. Syracuse was to be our last regular-season loss.

ROAD TO THE CHAMPIONSHIP

GAME THREE

Syracuse 38, Florida 21
September 21, 1991, Carrier Dome

SYRACUSE, N.Y. – Syracuse scored on the opening kickoff on a reverse carried 95 yards by Kirby DarDar, and the Orangemen went on to defeat the fifth-ranked Florida Gators 38-21 before 49,823 in the Carrier Dome.

"It was just a misdirection thing that we've worked on from the first day of practice," said Syracuse head coach Paul Pasqualoni. "We thought they would be coming hard, and we managed to get outside their containment."

After two possessions by the sputtering Florida offense went nowhere, Syracuse took advantage of a short punt and traveled 43 yards in six plays, scoring on a 10-yard run by David Walker off the option play. The Orangemen led 14-0 with the game less than four minutes old.

Florida got on the scoreboard in the first quarter on a seven-yard pass from Shane Matthews to Tre Everett, who injured his hamstring on the play and didn't return to the game. It was 14-7 at the end of the quarter.

In the second quarter, Syracuse quarterback Marvin Graves threw TD passes of 13 yards to Antonio Johnson and 36 yards to Qadry Ismail to pad their lead to 28-7.

The Gators got a lift when Matthews tossed a perfect 36-yard scoring pass in between two defenders to Aubrey Hill with only seven seconds remaining in the first half, cutting the margin to 28-14.

This appeared to give Florida an emotional lift as the Gators came out in the third quarter with Myrick Anderson's jarring hit that knocked the ball loose from Walker. Tony McCoy recovered at the Orangemen seven-yard line for the Gators.

Two plays later, Matthews hit Willie Jackson on a four-yard pass

SYRACUSE 38, FLORIDA 21

TEAM STATISTICS

	UF	SU
First Downs	20	27
Rushes-Yards	21-(-17)	29-250
Passing Yards	358	162
Passes	28-45-2	13-17-0
Total Offense	341	412
Penalties/Yards	8-59	6-40
Fumbles-Lost	2-0	2-1
Possession Time	23:59	36:01

Florida	7	7	7	0	– 21
Syracuse	14	14	0	10	– 38

INDIVIDUAL LEADERS

Rushing: Florida – Rhett 9-27, McClendon 3-8, McNabb 1-0, Ackerman 1-(-2), Matthews 7-(-50); Syracuse – Richardson 14-85, Walker 10-81 1TD, Lee 8-45, Womack 7-38 1TD

Passing: Florida – Matthews 27-43-347-2 Int, 3TD, Fox 1-2-11; Syracuse – Graves 13-16-162 2TD

Receiving: Florida – McClendon 5-72, Sullivan 5-65, Rhett 6-57, Hill 2-44 1TD, W. Jackson 2-39 1TD, Houston 3-32, McNabb 2-26, Randolph 2-17, Everett 1-7 1TD; Syracuse – Ismail 6-95, Johnson 2-23

to make it 28-21 less than five minutes into the half. The momentum appeared to be swinging in Florida's direction, but on its next possession, Syracuse turned it all around.

The Orangemen, alternating quarterbacks Graves and Doug Womack, moved with precision on an 11-play, 78-yard march to a touchdown, making it 35-21. Womack scored the TD on a three-yard run on an option play.

On their next possession Syracuse marched 72 yards and got a 25-yard field goal from John Biskup to put the game out of reach at 38-21.

Syracuse ran the option to perfection to gain 250 yards on 29 carries. Graves completed 13 of 16 passes for two touchdowns. For the Gators, Matthews completed 27 of 43 pass attempts for 347 yards and three touchdowns, but Florida rushed only 21 times for a school record minus 17 yards.

Syracuse stayed unbeaten at 3-0 while the Gators fell to 2-1. ■

13

BOUNCING BACK BIG

We put on the pads and did more hitting the week after the loss to Syracuse. We decided it was something we needed to do to sharpen up, and that it was worth the injury risk that goes along with increased contact.

It helped, and our senior leadership took over. By Saturday we were confident and fully ready to play a game that turned out to be one of our best total team performances of the season.

We had gotten away from the running game at Syracuse as a result of both our getting behind early and my bad play-calling. During the week we told our guys we were going to come out running the ball right at Mississippi State.

Our offensive line was fired up about that. Our running backs – Errict Rhett, Willie McClendon and Dexter McNabb – were excited and grinning all week about that style of play. It helped lead to very hard work on the practice field.

Somebody had sent me a copy of a book by former Michigan coach Bo Schembechler, and I decided to read it on the bus ride down to Orlando, where we were to play Mississippi State.

Although it was Mississippi State's home game, moving it to the Florida Citrus Bowl guaranteed extra money for the school. We certainly were glad they decided to come on down; it was just about like a home game for us, and Gators filled the stadium.

So on the ride down I read about Bo's coaching days at several schools, especially at the University of Michigan. I came to a chapter in which he talked about why his teams always have been known as running teams. He said running teams are generally tougher teams that can compete with hard-nosed defensive teams.

Although I don't totally agree with that philosophy, it was ironic to be reading it at that particular time and to be thinking, "You're right this week, Bo. The Gators need to bow their necks and take it to Mississippi State on the ground."

We started the game in the no-huddle offense, but we just basically were running the ball right and left, using a little bit of the unbalanced line. Mississippi State opened the game with five defensive backs on the field, having added the extra "nickel" back in anticipation of facing the usual Gator passing attack.

After we ran it up and down the field for a while, they changed back to their normal defense to try to stop the run.

Errict made some nice runs on our opening possession, and we had the ball at second-and-one on their 38-yard line. On that down you like to go deep, believing that if you're unsuccessful you can always come back and get the first down on the next play.

Shane made a beautiful throw to Tre Everett on a deep streak pattern. He caught it just inside the flag in the end zone, and we were up 7-0 with about a minute and a half gone in the first quarter.

Shane hung in the pocket and right before the half got hit with the hardest blow he was to take all year. We missed blocking a guy coming from wide left on Shane's blind side, and Shane was looking for Willie Jackson on a corner route. He stood there and made a perfect throw just before the pass rusher hit him right in the belly with his helmet, but he bounced right back up. It was a courageous performance by our quarterback.

This was a complete, solid team victory. Errict had more than 100 yards rushing, and our defense held Mississippi State to seven points. Tony McCoy came back to his hometown to play one of the finest games of his career at defensive tackle.

It was a solid game by our offense, defense and special teams, and we were back playing Gator football the way we had planned to play it all year.

That passage from Schembechler's book made me call even a few more running plays than I had planned. I think you do need to mix the run and the pass in there together. Even though your biggest chunks of yardage are going to come through the air, you have to let your team know you can run the ball against the defense.

Winning, successful teams – just about every one of them – have the ability to run as well as throw the ball. That Mississippi State game is where we got back to the combination of running and throwing that would carry us through the remainder of the year to the SEC championship.

A sad note from that game was when Rodney Stowers, Mississippi State's fine defensive lineman, suffered a broken leg when it appeared he got his cleats caught in the turf and fell wrong, or somebody fell into him. At the end of the game he was on the sidelines on crutches and appeared to be doing OK.

But some severe complications occurred after he returned to Mississippi, and he was rushed to the hospital. Just five days after the game, he passed away from a rare complication called fat embolism syndrome. It was a tragic day for his family and friends, Mississippi State and all of college football. Our players really felt terrible about it because they admired and respected Rodney as an athlete. Our thoughts, prayers and condolences went out to his family.

ROAD TO THE CHAMPIONSHIP

GAME FOUR

Florida 29, Mississippi State 7
September 28, 1991, Florida Citrus Bowl

ORLANDO, FLA. – Shane Matthews threw for over 300 yards and Errict Rhett rushed for 142 yards as Florida's 14th-ranked Gators handed 22nd-ranked Mississippi State a 29-7 defeat in front of 69,328 fans and a national WTBS-TV audience.

Matthews completed 22 of 35 passes for 322 yards and two TDs, giving him 36 for his career and tying him for third with Steve Spurrier on the all-time Gator list.

Rhett powered the first-half running game with 91 yards, which helped lead the Gators to a 17-0 lead by intermission. Overall, Florida had 517 yards of total offense, while holding the Bulldogs to 233 yards.

Florida scored on its first possession when Matthews connected with wide receiver Tre Everett on a 41-yard strike, the first pass attempt in a Rhett-dominated series of rushes. The 80-yard march resulted in the scoring toss only 1:50 into the game.

Following a 27-yard field goal by Arden Czyzewski early in the second quarter, the Gators made it 17-0 as Matthews hit Willie Jackson from 19 yards out with 3:17 remaining in the half.

Florida's defense, led by tackles Brad Culpepper and Tony McCoy, dominated the Bulldogs all afternoon, allowing only 77 yards rushing on 36 carries, while also registering three quarterback sacks, six tackles behind the line, two interceptions and seven QB hurries.

Culpepper was named SEC Defensive Player of the Week after a brilliant day in which he recorded 12 tackles, two QB sacks for a loss of 13 yards, two tackles behind the line of scrimmage for a loss of two yards and three quarterback hurries.

State's lone effective drive, 77 yards in 10 plays, resulted in a TD midway through the third quarter to cut the UF margin to 17-

FLORIDA 29, MISSISSIPPI STATE 7

TEAM STATISTICS

	UF	MSU
First Downs	27	6
Rushes-Yards	47-195	36-77
Passing Yards	322	156
Passes	22-37-1	9-19-2
Total Offense	517	233
Penalties/Yards	9-58	7-50
Fumbles-Lost	2-1	3-2
Possession Time	35:57	24:03

Florida	7	10	3	9 –	29
Mississippi St.	0	0	7	0 –	7

INDIVIDUAL LEADERS

Rushing: Florida – Rhett 27-142 1TD, McClendon 10-36, McNabb 5-28, Ackerman 3-10; Mississippi State – Williamson 6-31, Roberts 2-20, Prince 5-15 1TD

Passing: Florida – Matthews 22-35-322 1 Int, 2TD, Fox 0-2-0; Mississippi State – Plump 8-14-137, Jordan 1-5-19 2 Int

Receiving: Florida – Everett 4-112 1TD, W. Jackson 3-52 1TD, Rhett 6-38, Sullivan 3-45, McClendon 3-25, T. Jackson 2-28, Duncan 1-23; Mississippi State – Harrison 3-74, Davidson 2-46

7, but the Gators bounced back with a 37-yard Czyzewski field goal and a 64-yard, five-play drive that resulted in a Rhett TD run of three yards. Czyzewski's 23-yard field goal with 6:29 remaining ran the final count to 29-7.

Florida moved to 2-0 in the conference, while the Bulldogs dropped their second consecutive SEC contest. ∎

The next week we went to Baton Rouge, where LSU was really struggling in Coach Curly Hallman's first year. They had some problems while he was trying to instill some discipline into the team, and several of his players had gotten in trouble. For whatever reason, LSU was just not quite the team they normally are.

However, they were ready to play the Gators. The night we played them they were just about as good as any team we played in 1991. Thank goodness we were fully ready to play, because LSU came after us the same way Syracuse did. The Tigers played an excellent game, giving an all-out effort that we hadn't seen on tapes of their other games.

We entered the game in the frame of mind that if we were not ready physically, mentally and emotionally, the same thing could happen to us that happened at Syracuse. I felt very good about how we would play.

When we got to Baton Rouge, sportswriter Sam King of the *Baton Rouge Advocate*, said, "Steve, do you realize you are favored by about 21 or 22 points, the most points of any team that has played LSU here?"

That was a shock. To be favored at all in "Death Valley" is generally surprising, but to be favored by more than 20 points is unheard of and a bit scary.

Our game plan, offensively and defensively, was good. We wanted to mix up the run and the pass, and the defense intended to stop Todd Kinchen, their outstanding wide receiver, who is a game-breaker. We didn't think they could sustain the running game to beat us, but Kinchen was capable of giving them the big plays.

It turned out to be a game where we were very fortunate. LSU had some chances to hit TD passes, but the ball was just a little overthrown or something would happen where the quarterback just couldn't see the receiver.

We played very hard and escaped Tiger Stadium with a 16-0 victory. Errict Rhett ran hard and was dominating, and we managed to hit one big play for a touchdown.

At second-and-one on about our 40-yard line, an LSU player got hurt. While he was down being attended to and Shane Matthews was over near our bench, I thought of a play we didn't even have in the game plan.

It came to me suddenly that we'd been running Tre Everett on a deep crossing route, trying to clear out that deep area where he was heading, and the LSU defense had reacted. Tre had caught one or two earlier in the game, and I noticed their free safety was in the middle and chasing that route when we called 14 Pass, Z Cross, X Post. X is the split end, Y the tight end and Z the flanker. Tre was the Z, or flanker, running a crossing pattern on that play.

I yelled out to Shane to take a peek at the crosser (Tre) and then throw it as far as he could to the X-receiver. I grabbed Harrison Houston, who normally plays the Z position, and told him to jump in there at X. Harrison was the fastest receiver standing nearby who I could grab.

Shane called the play and sure enough, they were in their normal three-deep zone defense. Everett ran the crossing route, and the safety bit and stepped up about one step, but it was enough for Harrison to get behind him.

Shane made a perfect throw, one of his best of the season, and Harrison caught the ball diving in the back of the end zone, with the safety and another defensive back within a yard of him.

That got us to 13-0 at the time; we later added another field goal to make it 16-0 and then held on in the fourth quarter to preserve the shutout win.

It was a blue-collar, workmanlike victory in a tough arena, and as soon as the game was over, almost right after we had shaken hands with their players and coaches, we all were talking about Tennessee. The chatter in the locker room centered around the Vols finally coming to Gainesville the following Saturday.

It was obvious it might be a chore to keep our team from being totally ready to play Tennessee by the next day.

ROAD TO THE CHAMPIONSHIP

GAME FIVE

Florida 16, Louisiana State 0
October 5, 1991, Tiger Stadium

BATON ROUGE, LA. – Tony McCoy and the rest of his defensive teammates dominated LSU, and Arden Czyzewski's three field goals powered the Gator offense to lead Florida to a tough 16-0 victory.

McCoy had 11 tackles (nine solo), including five for a loss of 20 yards and two sacks for 12 yards in losses. Brad Culpepper pitched in with nine tackles, including two sacks for minus 21 yards. LSU gained only 35 yards rushing, and registered 166 yards of total offense on the night.

The shutout was Florida's second of the season against a conference school, the first time that has happened for the Gators since 1972. They have allowed only seven points in three league contests.

It was a defensive struggle all evening, with Florida's 220 passing yards and 16 points being their lowest of the season thus far. Florida had 404 yards of total offense, but had difficulty putting the ball into the end zone, settling for Czyzewski field goals in the first half.

Florida's first score came after a 37-yard drive stalled, and Czyzewski booted a 42-yard FG at the 5:29 mark of the first quarter.

In the second quarter, the Gators drove to the LSU four-yard line where they had a first-and-goal, but after three plays lost them three yards, Czyzewski came on to kick a 24-yarder to provide a 6-0 margin with 7:42 left in the half. Two possessions later the Gators drove from their own 40-yard line to the LSU two-yard line. However, with no time remaining on the clock, they settled for a 19-yard Czyzewski kick for a 9-0 halftime lead.

On their second possession of the second half, Florida gained 62

FLORIDA 16, LOUISIANA STATE 0

TEAM STATISTICS

	UF	LSU
First Downs	19	13
Rushes-Yards	39-184	32-35
Passing Yards	220	131
Passes	15-28-1	12-27-1
Total Offense	404	166
Penalties/Yards	9-68	6-68
Fumbles-Lost	1-1	0-0
Possession Time	32:53	27:07

Florida	3	6	7	0 –	16
LSU	0	0	0	0 –	0

INDIVIDUAL LEADERS

Rushing: Florida – Rhett 24-98, McNabb 8-46, McClendon 6-26, Matthews 1-14; LSU – Fuller 10-33, Loup 4-20

Passing: Florida – Matthews 15-28-220 1 Int, 1TD ; LSU – Daigle 5-15-65, Loup 7-12-131 1 Int

Receiving: Florida – Houston 3-77 1TD, Everett 2-35, Sullivan 2-35, W. Jackson 2-28, Rhett 3-26; LSU – Kinchen 3-39, Carter 3-29

yards on three plays, capped by a 35-yard touchdown pass from Shane Matthews to Harrison Houston, giving the Gators their only TD of the game and a 16-0 lead.

The Gator defense took over and kept LSU off the scoreboard the rest of the way as Florida went to 4-1 overall and 3-0 in the conference. LSU dropped to 1-3. ∎

14

VICTORY OVER VOLS

I f ever there was a game that needed no additional hype it was
our showdown against Tennessee in 1991, a struggle for the conference lead between two Top 10 teams on national television.

If that weren't enough newsworthy material, there was the fact
that the Vols had clobbered us the year before 45-3. We wanted to
redeem ourselves, and had been looking forward to this chance
for a year.

But the external hype came anyway. On Monday afternoon the
week of the game, Bill Arnsparger, our athletic director, called me
in and said he had just talked with Doug Dickey, former Gator
quarterback and head coach who is now athletic director at
Tennessee.

Coach Dickey told him they'd found out a former coach at
Tennessee, Jack Sells, had faxed down some play information to
Florida. Sells had been fired that summer by Dickey over some
violations. He was a good friend of our defensive coordinator,
Ron Zook, dating back to the days when they had coached
together there at Tennessee as assistants. Sells had faxed some
newspaper clippings out of the local paper to Zook. Later in the

week he faxed some plays we already knew about from scouting Tennessee. We already had spent countless hours watching game videotape of all of Tennessee's pass patterns.

I hadn't seen any of the faxed material, but Coach Zook said it was of absolutely no consequence or help; some of it was outdated old pass plays. In all my years of coaching, I've never seen a case in which a team's former coach could help you.

After the '91 season, I ran into Larry Lacewell, the exceptional defensive coordinator at Tennessee who has since joined the Dallas Cowboys. The conversation got around to how much one team learns about another from scouting and videos. I guarantee you Coach Lacewell knows just about everything about our offense. It wouldn't even help him much if we sent him our playbook. Larry told me, "Shoot, I even know your audibles. You use color audibles to change your plays."

It's not a big secret. Probably every team we play knows that. What you have to do when the other team knows some of your terminology is phony it up a little. If they are guessing, eventually they will get burned.

Anyhow, according to Coach Arnsparger, Doug Dickey was low-key about it on Monday. In fact, Doug joked that what they would do is to audible to the hitch pass and have the hitch-and-go already called. These are things you do when you think the other team knows something about your terminology.

It wasn't a big deal on Monday, and I didn't believe it would be much of one later until some sportswriters up in Knoxville made a big commotion about how this was really going to help the Gators. Then, of course, all the Florida writers had to ask me about it as the week went along. That was just part of having to do their job.

This was a week when I got involved with the defensive plans. Normally I don't do this except when we are playing a very good passing team. Tennessee was just that, with an outstanding pass receiver, Carl Pickens, and a solid quarterback in Andy Kelly. They were certainly an explosive passing team. I worked with our defensive coaches in coming up with some new schemes, such as one to disguise a blitz and one in which we would show blitz and then fall back into a zone defense.

I was in the office at 4:30 Monday morning watching their offensive and defensive tapes. Tuesday morning I was in there about 4:30 or 5. This is something I've been doing since coming to Florida.

As part of my weekly routine I try to relax quite a bit on Sundays. We'll watch the tape of the previous day's game, and try to get our corrections prepared. After I complete the regular 2 p.m. conference call with the media, I usually just take the afternoon off. I go home to try to rejuvenate myself, and maybe watch a pro game.

I'm usually drained by Sunday and am normally asleep by 8:30 or 9 o'clock. Then by 4 or so in the morning I'm wide awake, refreshed and ready to start preparing for the next opponent. I get a lot accomplished in the office by myself on Monday and Tuesday mornings, watching those tapes. By Wednesday I'm back to more normal office hours.

We give our team Sundays off in compliance with the NCAA rules setting limits on practice time, and we don't practice at all until Monday night. I learned while coaching at Duke University it is a good idea to give the players time on Monday to catch up on studies, attend class on what is normally a heavy class day, catch up on tutoring and get in their weight training. It also gives coaches the entire day to prepare for the next game.

What we saw on tape as we prepared for Tennessee confirmed what we already knew. They were coming to Gainesville with the most talented opposing team we would face there in my first two years with the Gators. Looking back, possibly the most talented teams we played in 1990 and 1991 were the two Tennessee teams.

The humiliating 1990 loss to the Vols hadn't stopped on the field. The Tennessee players imitated our "Gator Chomp," the band played "Rocky Top" in our ears all night long and the fans laughed and giggled at us. This was a game we had been pointing to all year long.

During the summer, at all my Gator Club stops, I told our

people that we needed to show Tennessee what crowd noise is all about when the Vols come to Florida Field. I told them that Vols head coach Johnny Majors had said the noise that night they played the Gators in Neyland Stadium was the loudest he had ever heard as a player or as a coach.

Sure enough, our fans didn't disappoint me or the team at all. In fact, when Coach Majors did his TV show the day after the game, he said Florida Field was the loudest visitor's stadium he had ever been in as a coach. I think the Gator crowd played a very important role in our victory. Tennessee had a couple of illegal procedure penalties and the quarterback dropped the snap from center and we recovered – these things happened because our crowd was into the game and behind our team.

We got off to a rough start. We might have been too eager to play and somewhat tense from the anticipation we all had felt about this opportunity to even the score for 1990. Before we could settle down, Shane got thrown for a safety, and we trailed 2-0. Then we almost had a disaster, which was averted by a great second effort by Willie Jackson.

Shane threw a pass to Willie. It was a little bit high, tipping off his hands and bouncing free only to be intercepted by a defensive back who had clear sailing to our end zone. Willie was off balance, but he lunged at the defender, knocked him off his feet and prevented a sure touchdown. Tennessee did not score on that possession.

When it all happens that fast, you don't know whether to be mad or glad. Emotions are on a roller-coaster ride for fans, players and coaches. Maybe that's why 60 minutes on a Saturday leave you so emotionally spent.

There were several bad memories of our trip to Neyland Stadium in 1990 that haunted us in the '91 game. One of them was their ability to run the draw play, something which killed us in their big victory. We decided we were not going to let them run the draw play up and down the field on us all night. We had a super plan to stop it, and they gained less than 50 yards rushing all night. We had our tackles lay back a little bit to stop that draw, and it worked so well that Tennessee just about abandoned running the ball as the game progressed.

There wasn't a bigger offensive play for us than the one we scored our first touchdown on to take a 7-2 lead. We never trailed after that, and it was a tremendous mental lift for our team. We were down to the one-yard line and it was fourth-and-goal. We had sputtered the previous week inside the 20 against LSU and wound up kicking three field goals.

For this game we had come up with a new short-yardage play, and I immediately went to it for this situation. We faked the sweep left, and Shane ran a naked bootleg back to his right with a couple of receivers out for a pass. Tennessee was expecting us to run and rushed everybody. Terrell Jackson, our tight end, was wide open; Shane just lobbed the ball to him for our first touchdown.

As the game went along, I could see that Coach Lacewell, one of the finest defensive coordinators in the nation, had spent a lot of time learning our pass patterns, then teaching them to his players. They were very well prepared and played a match-up zone coverage, in which their linebackers and defensive backs would drop into a zone and then head to where our receivers should be.

So we put in a couple of new wrinkles. Our receivers, instead of running a corner route, would break toward the post. We hit two or three nice gainers on this play, and made some crucial third-down conversions to keep the offense going.

This was the game in which Larry Kennedy came of age as a collegiate defensive back. There he was, out there as a freshman playing against Carl Pickens, one of the great receivers in college football. Larry broke up five passes intended for Pickens, all of them deep throws. At 5 foot 11, he went up in the air with Pickens, who is 6-4, and battled him every inch of the way.

Then he made the play that put the game away, sparking such an eruption of noise that it probably drowned out everything for blocks in every direction. We were nursing a 10-point lead at 28-18 with just over three minutes remaining. Everyone was anxious because of the way Tennessee's offense was going up and down the field. Kelly went back to pass and was hurried by freshman defensive end Kevin Carter, who was making his first start of the season. Larry was back there. He picked it off and scurried 44 yards in and around Tennessee players for a touchdown. When he put it in the end zone we knew the game was over.

It was special just to beat Tennessee, which has become an archrival in a short period of time, but it was extra special because it put us solidly in position to win the SEC. We were better than the teams we had left to play – Auburn, Georgia and Kentucky – and would be favored in each game. The championship was within sight.

An added bonus for the stretch run, and a good example of how the timing went right for us all season, was the return of defensive end Darren Mickell for the Tennessee game. He is 6 foot 5, 285 pounds, extremely quick and a talented athlete – one of the best defensive ends in the nation. He was just coming off an academic and disciplinary suspension, which required him to miss the first five games of the season. The week before, we had gotten our first major injury of the season when defensive end Mike Brandon hurt his knee playing LSU. He would be out for the rest of the season. Mickell replaced him and played the rest of the year.

When I think back on the 1991 season, the ability to remain almost injury-free, and to have an athlete like Mickell to replace Brandon, played a big part in our ability to be consistent week after week against the good teams on our schedule. Mickell's return would prove very significant as we made our stretch run toward the championship.

ROAD TO THE CHAMPIONSHIP

GAME SIX

Florida 35, Tennessee 18
October 12, 1991, Ben Hill Griffin Stadium

GAINESVILLE, FLA. – Florida ran its SEC record to 4-0 with a 35-18 victory over fourth-ranked Tennessee before a record crowd of 85,135.

The Gators jumped to a 21-12 lead at halftime, stretched it to a 16-point margin early in the second half, and then used a 44-yard TD interception return by freshman defensive back Larry Kennedy to put the Vols away in the final quarter.

Tennessee got off to a 2-0 lead early in the first quarter when defensive end Chucky Smith tackled Gator quarterback Shane Matthews in the end zone for a safety.

Florida came back with a 10-play drive, scoring on a pass from Matthews to tight end Terrell Jackson to give the Gators a 7-2 lead at the end of the quarter.

The Gators got a pair of touchdowns in the second quarter on a 29-yard pass from Matthews to Tre Everett and a four-yard run by Errict Rhett.

Tennessee countered with a scoring toss from quarterback Andy Kelly to split end Cory Fleming, and tacked on a 43-yard field goal by John Becksvoort just before the first half ended.

The Florida defense gave up more than 400 yards, but limited the high-scoring Vols to only one touchdown, intercepting Kelly three times. Tennessee's usually potent running game netted only 49 yards rushing.

In the second half Florida scored on a three-yard run by Rhett and Kennedy's interception return with 3:25 remaining in the game. Tennessee got only a pair of field goals by Becksvoort.

Matthews passed for 245 yards and two touchdowns on 20 of

FLORIDA 35, TENNESSEE 18

TEAM STATISTICS

	UT	UF
First Downs	28	18
Rushes-Yards	29-49	30-114
Passing Yards	392	246
Passes	33-56-3	21-37-3
Total Offense	441	360
Penalties/Yards	7-62	16-127
Fumbles-Lost	3-2	1-0
Possession Time	30:06	29:54

| Tennessee | 2 | 10 | 3 | 3 | – | 18 |
| Florida | 7 | 14 | 7 | 7 | – | 35 |

INDIVIDUAL LEADERS

Rushing: Tennessee – Hayden 7-23, Faulkner 2-16, Schuler 2-15, Stewart 8-0; Florida – Rhett 16-49 2TD, Matthews 11-36, McNabb 2-17, McClendon 1-12

Passing: Tennessee – Kelly 33-56-392 3 Int, 2TD; Florida – Matthews 20-35-245 2 Int, 2TD, Rhett 1-2-1

Receiving: Tennessee – Pickens 7-145, Faulkner 5-74, McCleskey 3-51, Fleming 2-10 1TD; Florida – W. Jackson 5-74, Houston 3-42, Everett 3-39 1TD, Rhett 3-35, McClendon 2-17, Hill 1-27, Duncan 1-9, T. Jackson 1-1 1TD, Randolph 1-1, Sullivan 1-1

35. He was intercepted twice. Rhett was the leading rusher on 16 carries for 49 yards and two touchdowns. Willie Jackson had five catches for 74 yards to top the receivers. ∎

15

WOUNDED
WAR EAGLES

After the physically and mentally exhausting win over Tennessee we were lucky to be playing Northern Illinois at our Homecoming. As it turned out, we played uninspired, lackadaisical football, which irritated me to no end.

Homecoming is a big deal at the University of Florida. We allow our seniors to ride in the parade and then take them to Gator Growl, Florida's annual homecoming show the night before the game, to be introduced to the crowd of about 70,000.

Brad Culpepper got up and told the crowd that this team was going to be known as the best team in Florida history. I told him to be careful about making those sort of statements in public because we hadn't accomplished it. Brad's fiance, Monica Frakes, was named Homecoming Queen that night.

I had hoped to play everyone in front of the Homecoming crowd. It should have been a nice day for the walk-ons, who work so hard in practice, to get out in front of 85,000 people and perform. They all were looking forward to it.

For a while we operated pretty much at ease, and it looked like the second half would be a fun time for our lesser-known players. But Northern Illinois didn't want to be humiliated, and they had a good game plan to hold the ball, make first downs and eat up the clock.

We helped them by standing around and watching. We just sputtered; it was impossible to get the attention of our players, although we talked to them pretty good on the sideline.

I understand that there are some games where you reach down and get extra emotion, and that you can't draw it out at that level every Saturday. However, when there are only 11 or 12 games to play in a season, you should have enough pride to get prepared to play as well as you can each week.

Even though we won the game 41-10, I chewed out the team pretty good after the game. I felt like I couldn't allow them to be content with such a lackluster performance. My reaction was the culmination of an afternoon when I simmered so long over the lack of effort that it finally reached the boiling point.

In the media briefing later, I told the reporters that I had watched the cheerleaders and Gator Dazzlers dance team at Gator Growl Friday night, and they did all their routines in perfect unison. But we couldn't even get four guys to line up correctly behind the ball. It was terrible.

Shane Matthews said I was on his tail all afternoon. He added: "I deserved it." And Tony McCoy, the fine senior defensive tackle, said, "I've never felt this bad after a win."

ROAD TO THE CHAMPIONSHIP

GAME SEVEN

Florida 41, Northern Illinois 10
October 19, 1991, Ben Hill Griffin Stadium

GAINESVILLE, FLA. – Despite a performance that drew the wrath of head coach Steve Spurrier, Florida still managed 604 yards of total offense against outmanned Northern Illinois to win its Homecoming game 41-10 before a crowd of 83,708.

FLORIDA 41, NORTHERN ILLINOIS 10

TEAM STATISTICS

	NI	UF
First Downs	14	28
Rushes-Yards	49-155	28-133
Passing Yards	88	471
Passes	5-14-0	29-45-0
Total Offense	243	604
Penalties/Yards	7-37	13-73
Fumbles-Lost	3-3	0-0
Possession Time	32:25	27:35

Northern Illinois	0	0	0	10 –	10
Florida	14	14	0	13 –	41

INDIVIDUAL LEADERS

Rushing: Northern Illinois – Dach 28-74, McKinney 8-38; Florida – Rhett 12-55 2TD, McNabb 7-45, McClendon 3-21 1TD, Ackerman 2-6, Matthews 3-4, Randolph 1-2

Passing: Northern Illinois – Rugal 2-3-51 1TD, McKinney 3-11-37; Florida – Matthews 21-34-336 2TD, T. Dean 5-7-103 1TD, Fox 3-4-32

Receiving: Northern Illinois – Roberts 2-18 1TD; Florida – W. Jackson 6-127 1TD, Sullivan 6-78, Glenn 2-66 1TD, Houston 3-57 1TD, Hill 2-36, Bolduc 2-29, Duncan 1-24, McClendon 2-18, T. Jackson 2-12, McNabb 1-12, Franklin 1-8, Rhett 1-4

The Gators had 13 penalties and converted only one of 10 third-down attempts while jumping off to a 28-0 halftime lead and coasting the rest of the way.

Florida's defense held the Huskies scoreless until 5:10 remained in the contest and surrendered only 243 yards, but the offense sputtered despite gaining a school-record 471 passing yards.

The Gators scored in the first half on a one-yard run by Errict Rhett, a two-yard run by Willie McClendon and passes from Shane Matthews to Harrison Houston for 18 yards and to Willie Jackson for 32. Rhett scored again in the final quarter on a two-yard plunge, and reserve quarterback Terry Dean found walk-on wide receiver Kevin Glenn on an 18-yard touchdown strike.

The Gator defense was led by Brad Culpepper, Tim Paulk and Fee Bartley. Punter Shayne Edge boomed five punts for an average of 49.4 yards to continue his march toward All-SEC honors. ■

We had an open date the next week, with the Auburn and Georgia weekends staring us in the face afterward. It was time to forget Northern Illinois and move on in a positive manner.

Playing at Auburn has long been an enigma for Gator teams. The first time we were able to beat them at Jordan-Hare Stadium (it was Cliff Hare Stadium then) was in 1973. The team I was on in 1965 went in there as favorites, and came away losers after a series of weird big plays perpetrated by the inspired Tigers.

Being favored in that stadium brings no guarantee of success. We coaches knew that in 1991, and so did our team.

Auburn was struggling a little bit, and had some off-field problems with a former player going public with claims of NCAA violations. This appeared to be damaging their morale and taking focus away from the season. But we knew it was a crucial game and Coach Pat Dye would be priming them for the big upset of the Gators.

We had gotten word that some recruits had been told by the Auburn staff that if they could come to visit for only one game, they should watch the Florida game, because they were going to kick the Gators' tail.

Our 48-7 victory the year before in Gainesville, the worst defeat an Auburn team has ever suffered at the hands of Florida, was also one of the worst in Coach Dye's career, maybe the worst.

Auburn had issued a challenge, we told our players, that they couldn't wait until we came up to their place so they could get even for the 1990 loss. This would be a game that would show what we are made of; that we're a different breed of Gators now. We wanted our team to show everyone we're not like former Gator teams. There were no excuses, and there wasn't a reason in the world why we shouldn't go over there and beat Auburn if we gave it all we had.

We didn't even mention Auburn until after a scrimmage on Friday of the off-week. We just tried to refine our offense and defense and get some younger players ready to play for the stretch run of the season. There was a nice scrimmage on Friday, something we don't normally do, but I let the first teams butt heads against each other for about 10 minutes to get some excitement going, and it worked.

We stayed in LaGrange, Georgia, about 50 minutes up the interstate from Auburn; there were many Gator fans around there and also at nearby Callaway Gardens. We sell all 7,500 tickets we get for this game each year. Talk about a stadium full of orange and blue when these two teams meet each other – Auburn shares our school colors.

The kickoff would be at 4 p.m. in order to fit the ESPN-TV schedule for that day, and I had my normal game-day jog of a few miles. It is a great way to relax, and I never miss it at home or away.

At home Carl Franks always jogs with me, and John Reaves has missed it only once or twice. My wife, Jerri, jogs when we are on the road, but at home she is too busy getting the kids ready, making the fried chicken and sandwiches for after the game and with whatever other details wives have to attend to on a football Saturday.

Dr. Nick Cassisi, our faculty representative who was instrumental in hiring me, jogged with us that day for the first time. Hopefully, we'll make that a tradition on the road.

A 4 o'clock kickoff meant breakfast would be at 9 a.m., offensive and defensive meetings with the players at 9:30 and the pregame meal at noon.

In my meeting with the offense I was going over plays we wanted to use. About 10 minutes into the meeting our wide receiver coach, Dwayne Dixon, came into the room and sat in the back.

Afterward, I asked him if he had known there was to be a meeting. He said he just overslept.

I said, "It's 9:30 on game day, and you can't wake up for a meeting?"

"No sir," was his reply.

Dwayne is one of our most relaxed coaches. In fact, he is one of the most relaxed coaches I have ever met, and he can sleep no matter if it's game day or recruiting day or whatever. One day I'm going to ask his wife, Sandra, if he was at their wedding on time.

I couldn't get too upset with Dwayne. I used to fall asleep on the way to the stadium before games. I would take a nice little nap if the stadium was a 40-minute bus ride away.

When we got to Auburn, it was cool and definitely sweater weather on sort of a raw early-November day in Alabama. It was the kind of day that makes you appreciate living in Florida.

Out on the field before the game I talked to my good buddy Pat Sullivan, who coached the Auburn quarterbacks and is now the head coach at TCU. We discussed our December trip to New York, when he would be inducted into the National Football Hall of Fame. It's a trip we make each year because there is also a reunion of Heisman Trophy winners in conjunction with the Hall of Fame ceremonies. Pat, who won the Heisman in 1972, is a great guy and a good coach, and I wish him the best at TCU.

Coach Dye came over and said hello. We're a lot different as coaches, but you can't deny the success he's had doing it his way. His players play hard for him, and I have tremendous respect for him.

My good friend, Tom McEwen, sports editor of the *Tampa Tribune*, came over later. We have known each other since I was a player in 1963 and right on through my coaching days with the Tampa Bay Bandits and with the Gators.

Tom told me Coach Dye had just told him Auburn was going to win the game if they could stop Errict Rhett. I don't know why Pat told him that, but maybe he hoped Tom would tell me what he said and that I would somehow react to it.

I didn't pay much attention to it and didn't even mention it to my team. Sometimes opposing coaches say things to people knowing they will repeat it to you and hoping you will tell your team. Our team was ready to play and didn't need anything else said at that point. I just don't pay much attention to pregame chatter and really don't like to talk to the opposing coach except for a quick, polite hello.

The 1991 Kentucky game was a good example of pregame coaching strategy. Coach Bill Curry came across the field and started telling me how much the Gators deserved the championship, and that this was going to be a wonderful day of celebration for the Florida people, and so forth. I couldn't figure out why in the world he was saying all those flowery things, and even told him we would have to beat them first.

It dawned on me in the fourth quarter, when they were about to knock us out of the Sugar Bowl. He knew they were ready to play and believed they would upset the Gators, and he had hoped to lull us to sleep.

Those comments didn't have anything to do with it, but the way his team played sure did.

So Pat's remarks at Auburn were forgotten, and we went through our normal dressing room routine before the opening kickoff. We are pretty much businesslike at that time, because I believe emotional talks right before a game have a tendency to fade out very quickly.

I think the night before the game is the time to give an emotional talk, because I believe it will sustain you through the game. Jerry Anderson had been assigned this game as the scout, and he gave a talk Friday night that had the team fired up, and they stayed fired up.

That was good. I thought we were the better team; and if we

played hard and kept our poise, Auburn had very little chance to beat us – maybe they couldn't even keep it close. And that's pretty much what happened.

We built the lead on passing in the first half. We moved Willie Jackson to the X, or split end, position, where he hadn't played before. I had told him right before the game to be ready for his big day. The way Auburn plays, there would be a good opportunity to throw a lot of balls his way.

We put him there because we know he can catch; if Shane gets the ball in the area, Willie's going to catch it. He caught 10 passes in the first half and 12 for 157 yards in the game.

When Auburn came back to within seven points at 17-10 in the third quarter, there might have been some apprehension among the 8,000 or so Gators there, but we were not worried. The coaches and players were poised in that arena where fate had been unkind over the years.

We were a stronger team physically, and I decided to use that strength, to go to the running game and take Auburn out of it. Errict Rhett ran for almost 200 yards. After he scored late in the third quarter, the Auburn fans started leaving the stadium.

I've never seen that before at Auburn: strong, loyal fans leaving such an important game. But we did have a big lead and our defense was outstanding, so maybe it was out of respect for us that they didn't think Auburn could come back.

The only negative of the game was our kickoff coverage, which was lousy – as it had been all season. On five of their first six possessions in the first half they started on our side of the field, but they scored only three points.

Even the long bus ride in the dark back to the Columbus, Georgia, airport wasn't too bad after our fourth win in history at Jordan-Hare.

ROAD TO THE CHAMPIONSHIP

GAME EIGHT

Florida 31, Auburn 10
November 2, 1991, Jordan-Hare Stadium

AUBURN, ALA. – Florida's defense overcame poor field position for most of the game and dominated the Auburn offense as the Gators posted their fifth consecutive SEC victory of the season with a convincing 31-10 win.

Despite an average field position starting at their own 42-yard line in the first half, the Tigers could score only three points in the half, while Florida got two touchdowns and a field goal to jump out to a commanding 17-3 lead at intermission.

The Gator offense, led by Willie Jackson's 12 receptions for 157 yards and one touchdown, gained 468 yards and had 30 first downs, compared with Auburn's 12 first downs, 195 yards of offense and four turnovers.

Tim Paulk led the Florida defense with 11 tackles, two behind the line for a loss of six yards, while Will White intercepted a pair of passes to raise his career total to 13, tying the UF school record.

Shane Matthews had an exceptional day in the frigid fall weather, with 20 completions in 36 attempts, good for 264 yards and two touchdowns. It was the fifth time he has completed 20 or more passes this season, and his 13th consecutive 200-yard passing game. Errict Rhett ran for 106 yards on 26 carries, his third 100-yard game of the season and the seventh of his career.

Matthews set the tone for the day on the opening possession as the Gators marched 78 yards in 12 plays to score when he ran 10 yards for his first TD of the season. Arden Czyzewski's 26-yard field goal in the second quarter upped the margin to 10-0, then the Tigers kicked a field goal to make it 10-3 before an 11-yard pass from Matthews to Jackson gave Florida a 17-3 lead at halftime.

FLORIDA 31, AUBURN 10

TEAM STATISTICS

	UF	AU
First Downs	30	12
Rushes-Yards	46-198	29-85
Passing Yards	270	110
Passes	21-37-2	14-25-3
Total Offense	468	195
Penalties/Yards	6-61	6-55
Fumbles-Lost	2-2	1-1
Possession Time	25:37	34:23

Florida	7	10	7	7	–	31
Auburn	0	3	7	0	–	10

INDIVIDUAL LEADERS

Rushing: Florida – Rhett 26-106 1TD, Matthews 7-41 1TD, McNabb 7-29, McClendon 6-24; Auburn – Mounds 12-70, Frazier 5-15

Passing: Florida – Matthews 20-36-264 2 Int, 2TD, Fox 1-1-6; Auburn – White 14-25-110 3 Int, 1TD

Receiving: Florida – W. Jackson 12-157 1TD, Duncan 2-30, Houston 1-28 1TD, Hill 2-26, Rhett 3-23, Sullivan 1-6; Auburn – Casey 3-60 1TD, Hall 3-23, Baxter 2-25

The Tigers scored in a hurry in the third quarter, capping a short drive with a 30-yard TD pass from QB Stan White to wide receiver Herbert Casey, but that was the end of the line for their offense.

Florida added a pair of touchdowns on a 28-yard pass from Matthews to Harrison Houston and a three-yard run by Rhett to make the final score 31-10. ∎

16

BRING ON THE DAWGS

Some close friends of mine were sitting in a popular restaurant in Jacksonville Friday night before the 1991 Florida-Georgia game. A little old lady dressed in red and black started a conversation about Florida's chances the next day against her Bulldogs.

She said something like this: "Sure, Florida beat us in 1984 when they were on probation and last year when they knew they weren't eligible to win the title, but they have never beaten us when it counts, when the championship is on the line."

This confidence had built up over the years, as Georgia teams portrayed as less talented but "wanting it more" had fairly consistently beaten Florida teams. It had gotten to the point that Georgia fans, players, coaches and support staff regarded the Gator Bowl as their home stadium for the annual game with the Gators.

Not long after I was named head coach at Florida, several Gator fans, boosters and others came to me and repeated what was on far too many minds: We need to quit playing Georgia in Jacksonville. We just can't beat them there, and we need to go home-and-home with them to give us a 50/50 chance to win.

I already had thought about this great series and concluded: Why wouldn't it be an advantage for us to play Georgia in our state in a stadium named the Gator Bowl? Heck, we *are* the Gators. This is a road game for Georgia and almost a home game for us.

Another excuse went by the boards when we ripped out the Astroturf at Florida Field, eliminating the theory that Astroturf teams don't play well on grass.

Our players now fully understand that they are not responsible for past Gator failures in Jacksonville, that they are as talented as Georgia and that this is a home game for us. Why not beat Georgia in Jacksonville?

The important fact for Gators to remember is that the game is played on Florida soil. Usually, both teams are talented and capable of winning a big game like this, but we have the home field edge every year. The generally accepted image of the two teams, however, is that Florida has vastly superior athletes and talent compared with Georgia. Vince Dooley did a masterful job of creating this mind-set over the last quarter-century as Georgia's head coach.

This notion has been built up in the media until most people think it is factual. Newspaper articles leading up to the 1991 game mentioned that the Bulldogs did not have as much talent as Florida as usual, but that for some reason they probably would play harder. Sportswriters predicted that their quarterback might lead Georgia down the field for another last-second victory, like those that have happened so often in Jacksonville.

During the summer a friend of mine from Jacksonville, Merrill Poole, saved an article from *Georgia Football Report* by Harry Cain. Merrill sent me the clipping Monday of the week of the Georgia game.

Georgia Football Report said that the Gators have a lot of talent, but do not have the right team mentality; and that we assume the wins will come. Cain wrote that Georgia would punish the overrated Gators for making assumptions. The Bulldogs were ready to win the SEC crown, he concluded.

Another reason Georgia would win the championship, according to the report, was that they had signed more quality players over the past five years than any other team in the conference. Florida was down around fifth in his analysis.

After I received this publication, I asked Norm Carlson to see if he could find an article about what Vince Dooley had said before the 1985 game, when Florida was ranked number one in the nation. Sure enough, Coach Dooley had said during the week of the game that this was the finest Florida team he had ever seen. Georgia went on to beat Florida 24-3.

Coach Ray Goff said the exact same thing the week of the 1991 game: "This is the best Florida team I've seen since I've been at Georgia." He went on to talk about Florida's super athletes and great talent at every position. He claimed that many of our starters would be playing in the NFL the next season, although it turned out we didn't have a player picked in the first three rounds of the draft.

Coach Goff said his Bulldogs were the underdogs and didn't have nearly the talent that Florida had on its roster. Their team would just have to play tougher and smarter and want to win more than the Gators; that is their theme each year.

The subject came up on my Thursday night TV/radio call-in show on SportsChannel. People wanted to know my opinion on these compliments that flow each year. I mentioned that according to the Georgia report, the Bulldogs had finished first in the conference in recruiting over the past five years. They have fine players just like we have fine players.

I told the audience we are sort of tired of their always saying that they are so outmanned and such big underdogs. Also, we have learned that the only time some of our opponents say good things about us is the week of the game. They sure don't talk about us that way during recruiting season or over the summer. Our players have to understand they shouldn't get carried away with flattering press clippings, because the intent is to make us complacent and get us a little soft. This has worked for Vince Dooley in the past but, hopefully, we're a lot smarter than that now. We respect Georgia and their ability.

After the game, a member of the media brought up the comments on my call-in show. My answers to the ensuing questions from the media were later interpreted by some people as criticism of Coach Goff's coaching ability, but that certainly was not my intent.

I responded to the media questions, saying that coaches at Florida were tired of Georgia coaches saying what great players we have and that their players don't measure up to our players. I again mentioned that Georgia had finished first in recruiting over the past five years and Florida had finished fifth, according to the *Georgia Football Report,* and that the Bulldogs have plenty of outstanding players, as does Florida. If their recruiting is that good, then you have to wonder what happened to these athletes after they got to Georgia. They have had attrition for academic and disciplinary reasons, but they are still a well-coached, talented team.

I would just like to see a year when the players of both teams get to play the game without all the fanfare about how much better one team is than the other. Both teams are good, and this rivalry should continue to be one of the best in college football.

Our players have matured in their attitudes toward pregame flattery and are now able to see through it. They were emotional and upset about the praise coming out of Athens, and it helped them get ready for the game. We had one of the best weeks of practice that we'd had all season.

The weather was good all week until Friday; by the time we reached the Marriott Sawgrass in Jacksonville, the howling wind and the dampness were pushing the temperature down. At kick-off time Saturday in the Gator Bowl, on the banks of the St. Johns River, it was cold. Big Ten football fans would have thought they were in Ann Arbor, Michigan, or Columbus, Ohio. The wind chill factor, I was told, got into the 20s and it was near freezing on the thermometer in the second half. The swirling wind coming off the river concerned us in the warmups.

But nothing bothered Shane Matthews that day. We really got control of the game on our first possession, a 74-yard scoring drive on 11 plays. Shane threw a five-yard touchdown pass to Willie Jackson, who jumped and brought it down with the Georgia defensive back hanging on his waist. They did come back and kick a field goal to make it 7-3, but that was the closest they would get all afternoon, as the Gators played a near-perfect game offensively and defensively.

The second quarter, for some reason, has been our most productive 15 minutes in most games. Against Georgia we scored 21 points to put the game away, and did it on drives of 71, 70 and 96 yards. That last one must have been a back-breaker for the Bulldogs.

They had us pinned near the goal and probably thought a punt into that wind would set them up in great position. Instead, Errict Rhett's running got us some room. Then Shane hit Alonzo Sullivan on a little sideline route, and Alonzo juked the defensive back almost off his feet, taking the ball 61 yards down the sideline for a touchdown.

Shane got great protection, and he picked Georgia apart. He was 22 of 32, passing for 303 yards and four touchdowns. Rhett got 125 yards rushing, the fourth time he had gone over the 100-yard mark that season. I guess some of the Georgia people thought we had run up the score, because reserve quarterback Brian Fox threw a 24-yard touchdown pass in the final quarter. But we are going to run our offense no matter who is in the game. I don't believe it's fair to reserves to tell them that they are getting a chance to play, but they can't do anything. We'll try to play 60 minutes of football each week, and we'll try to score when we get the ball.

This victory gave us a share of the conference championship for the first time officially in school history. The players were almost matter-of-fact about it. The celebration was joyous, but not unrestrained. They had already started thinking about Kentucky, and the chance to win it all at home in front of our fans.

GAME NINE

Florida 45, Georgia 13
November 9, 1991, Gator Bowl

JACKSONVILLE, FLA. – Quarterback Shane Matthews set an SEC record with his ninth career 300-yard passing game and tied another with his 24th TD pass, leading Florida past Georgia 45-13 in front of 81,679 to clinch at least a share of the Gators' first official conference title.

Matthews connected for four touchdown passes, two of them to sophomore wide receiver Willie Jackson, and the Gator defense held the Bulldogs to 25 yards rushing and only 220 yards of total offense.

Florida's domination of the first half was total as they ran up 314 yards on 37 plays, an average of 8.49 yards per snap. The Gators led at halftime 28-6 as Matthews threw three touchdown passes, and Errict Rhett ran 13 yards for another score.

Matthews' TD strikes were for four yards to Jackson, 36 to Harrison Houston and 61 to Alonzo Sullivan, who took a short sideline toss and made an outstanding move to fake Bulldog defensive back George Wynn out of position and race down the sideline for his first career TD in four years of competition.

The second half was more of the same as the Gators padded their lead to 25 points at 38-13. Georgia got its lone TD of the game late in the third quarter, but Matthews quickly responded with a nine-yard scoring pass early in the final quarter. The touchdown pass gave Matthews 24 for the season, tying him for the SEC mark set by John Reaves, the former Gator All-American and current tight-end coach, in 1969.

The final score of the game came with 6:22 remaining when Florida capped a 43-yard drive with a 24-yard pass from reserve quarterback Brian Fox to Jackson. It was Jackson's third TD grab against the Bulldogs, tying him for the school single-game record.

It also gave the standout sophomore 10 TDs for the season,

FLORIDA 45, GEORGIA 13

TEAM STATISTICS

	UF	UGA
First Downs	29	14
Rushes-Yards	43-185	25-25
Passing Yards	327	195
Passes	23-33-0	18-35-1
Total Offense	512	220
Penalties/Yards	10-86	7-73
Fumbles-Lost	0-0	1-0
Possession Time	34:27	25:33

Florida	7	21	3	14	–	45
Georgia	3	3	7	0	–	13

INDIVIDUAL LEADERS

Rushing: Florida – Rhett 25-124 1TD, McNabb 6-32, Matthews 4-10, Bilkie 4-6, Ackerman 1-6, McClendon 2-3, Mangus 1-4; Georgia – Hearst 15-39, Strong 3-11

Passing: Florida – Matthews 22-32-303 4TD, Fox 1-1-24 1TD; Georgia – Zeier 18-35-195 1 Int, 1TD

Receiving: Florida – W. Jackson 7-80 3TD, Houston 6-93 1TD, Sullivan 3-86 1TD, Rhett 3-20, McNabb 1-29, Duncan 1-7, Randolph 1-5, C. Dean 1-7; Georgia – Hastings 5-64 1TD, Marshall 5-55, Hearst 4-48

tying him for second place with Wes Chandler (1976) and Ernie Mills (1990).

The win improved Florida's record to 8-1 overall and a perfect 6-0 in the conference. The Gators not only clinched at least a share of their first official championship, they also became the first team in school history to win their first six league games in a season, and the first to score 30 or more points against Georgia in back-to-back seasons. ∎

17

'THE DRIVE' WINS IT

Kentucky almost won their 1991 game against Florida in Gainesville. That is a more accurate way of putting it than to say Florida almost lost it.

We had a lot of things to play for: our first official championship, seven conference wins in a season, the Sugar Bowl bid and a national ranking. But Kentucky, an unheard-of 36-point underdog in an SEC game, came in mad and ready to beat us. Coach Bill Curry and his staff put a wonderful game plan together that gave them a chance to win it, and they did everything but win it.

They were 0-5 in the conference, last in the league in defense and next to last in offense. We had clinched a share of the title the week before against Georgia. It looked like a mismatch on paper. It wasn't.

I did a lot of things wrong that week that hurt our team's preparation. It started early in the week, when SEC Commissioner Roy Kramer called and asked if we had any problems with playing Miami in the Sugar Bowl.

I should have told him we weren't even in the Sugar Bowl yet and needed to be concerned about beating Kentucky first; but the bowls were being put together at that time, and he said the Sugar Bowl wanted Miami and needed to know if we had any objections.

I told him that's who we should be playing if we beat Kentucky. We want to play Miami if at all possible, and with both teams in the top five, the game in New Orleans could have national championship implications.

I then called my friend, Dennis Erickson, the coach at Miami, and told him we needed to play each other in New Orleans. He said he'd like to do that, but he wasn't sure the Sugar Bowl wanted his team, and that his athletic director probably would want them to stay in Miami for the Orange Bowl to make more money if they beat FSU that coming Saturday.

Personally, I wish we had a playoff system. Then coaches wouldn't get involved in the politics and lobbying to get the various teams into the various bowls. The newly formed bowl alliance makes virtually automatic where the various conference champions and runners-up will go. Maybe this will help eliminate the need for politicking.

I made a big mistake even talking about another team the week of our game against Kentucky for the conference championship. I told the team to let me do the talking about the possibilities with the Sugar Bowl and Miami and to keep their minds on Kentucky.

At that time I had no idea whether or not Notre Dame already had been locked up as the Sugar Bowl visiting team. The only conversation I had on the subject was the one with Commissioner Kramer.

Well, things got out of hand, and the media wanted to talk about Miami and the Sugar Bowl all week long. My mind deviated from the game and it almost cost us the championship outright. If we had lost that game, Alabama would have been the Sugar Bowl representative, because they would have been higher ranked than us.

Finally, after a couple more days of the media talking about Miami and our players from Miami talking about how they would love to play the 'Canes, we started getting ready for Kentucky.

Brad Culpepper had said after the Georgia game, in response to a question, that "playing Kentucky is like a gimme putt in golf, but I've missed gimme putts before." As you would expect, by the time it got to the Wildcats, the quote read: "Culpepper Says Kentucky a Gimme," as if they didn't have enough ammunition with the really absurd 36-point underdog label.

The game was like two totally different games. There was the first half, and then there was the second half. Two games in one.

Thank goodness Tre Everett was healthy and ready to play. He made two of the most unbelievable catches under pressure I've witnessed, and they turned out to be even bigger than they looked at the time.

On the first one, the free safety got his back turned on a ball underthrown at the Kentucky 22; Tre plucked the ball right off his pads and was bumped by another defensive back. Somehow he held onto the ball and got his balance to romp into the end zone for a 65-yard touchdown.

The next catch was a 33-yard TD; he took the ball right out from between the defensive back's hands in the air in the end zone. Incredible plays, both of them.

Our first touchdown had been a pass to Aubrey Hill, our gifted little receiver from Miami. He is our fifth receiver in the no-back offense and we don't have a letter to denote his position on the field. So we just call it "Aubrey Post," "Aubrey Under," "Aubrey Corner" and so forth. He scored on "Aubrey Under."

On second-and-five in the second quarter at the Kentucky 15 we came up with a play we had worked on for two years. It's a screen back to the quarterback. We throw it out to a wide receiver, who looks downfield a moment and then throws it back to quarterback Shane Matthews.

We tried it at FSU in 1990. The throw back was a little low and Shane dropped it. If he hadn't, he would have had all kinds of open field to run. It is a play we used at Duke, and it worked almost every time. This play is usually good for about 25 to 30 yards, so if you run it down around the 20 you have a good chance to score.

It worked perfectly. All the Kentucky players chased the lateral pass. Alonzo Sullivan, who was a high school quarterback, caught it and made a beautiful pass back to Shane, who romped in easily behind our offensive linemen.

We were up 28-3 and there were more than 11 minutes left in the first half. I looked around and told one of the assistant coaches we could score a bundle at this pace. Well, it didn't continue at that pace. In fact we didn't score again until late in the fourth quarter.

I have to give Kentucky credit. They didn't panic; they kept mixing up the run and the pass. Although our defense was playing pretty well, Kentucky would convert on all the third downs. Third and six, they would make it. Third and eight, they would make it. Third and four, they would make it. It didn't matter what the distance was.

That drive used up about eight minutes of the clock. Then they got to fourth-and-five and attempted a fake field goal. The receiver was wide open, and the ball was fairly well thrown, but Del Speer got back there and barely tipped it away to save a touchdown. We didn't know at the time how important that extra-effort deflection would turn out to be in that game.

We went in ahead 28-6 at halftime and tried to keep our players focused on continuing to do what we'd done in the first half. However, some of our players' minds were drifting to the postgame celebration in which they already were taking part mentally. There had been a lot written about the ceremony planned for after the game. Hats and T-shirts already had been made up declaring Florida 1991 SEC Champions.

In the second half we moved the ball well, but we threw an interception in the end zone, Errict lost his first fumble of the year and it was just something here, something there preventing us from getting any points.

Then Kentucky started moving the ball at will against us. Our defense was confused by their excellent offensive plan. The quarterback was running the option, he was dropping back to pass and then running. They had a little sprint-out passing game that we couldn't contain.

We were certainly one of the best defensive teams in the conference, but in the second half we not only couldn't stop Kentucky, we couldn't even slow them down.

They narrowed the score to 28-26 with almost eight minutes remaining. There were some really nervous people around, including me on the sideline. I'm not supposed to act nervous, but my visor was taking a beating.

I got the offensive guys together and told them we needed to drive this clock out and go win this thing if we truly are champions; if we didn't do it, there would be no excuses.

The pressure was right smack-dab on our offense. Our defense was struggling, and the SEC championship hopes had come down to this.

I'll never forget "The Drive" and the tension that went with it.

On first down from our 29 after the kickoff we were penalized 17 yards when offensive guard Hesham Ismail got his hand under the defensive tackle's facemask two yards behind our line of scrimmage. We were then first-and-27 on our 12-yard line with more than seven minutes remaining in the game.

We completed passes to Errict and Alonzo and got it to third-and-six. Now came one of the biggest plays of the season. Errict was the intended receiver, and at the end of his route he had the option of breaking left, breaking right or turning around and hooking back toward the line of scrimmage. We messed up the pass protection and an unblocked Kentucky lineman was heading straight toward Shane.

Shane had to get rid of the ball. He guessed that Errict would turn around and he threw it before Errict had made his move. A Kentucky linebacker was about three yards behind Errict, and if Errict had decided to go either left or right, the ball would have hit the linebacker right in the numbers.

Fortunately, Errict turned around and had his hands up and ready, and the ball immediately hit him in the hands. He made the catch, carried the linebacker about two yards and got the first down.

From there we ran it every down. Willie McClendon came in for Errict on one play, a second-and-ten, and made a super run, faking his way past a defender and taking it 17 yards down to the 20.

We scored on third-and-two when Errict ran a sweep around the weak side. He got hit right around the goal line, spun, and fell with the ball in his left arm. He was lying flat, straddling the goal line, with the ball just over the line for the touchdown. If the ball had been in his right arm, it would have been short of the goal line.

If it had been in the other arm, I would have been standing there with fourth-and-one, a two-point lead and just over two minutes left while trying to decide what in the heck to do. I'm glad I didn't have to make that call, but for those who wonder – we would have tried to run for it.

"The Drive" took 5:30 off the clock, and we scored with 2:22 left in the game.

We escaped a good Kentucky team 35-26 to win the championship. It was so important for the Gators, for everyone who ever had attended the university or pulled for them.

It was important for all the faculty, students and everyone who ever was associated with us. Now the monkey is off our back. No longer can other schools or the media ridicule the Gators for never winning the championship, or say we can win it only when we're on probation.

As the game faded to the last few seconds, offensive linemen Tony Rowell and Hesham Ismail grabbed me and carried me to the middle of the field. I had told my players that the only time they could carry me off the field was after we won a championship. They carried me off the field in Lexington after the Kentucky game in 1990, and again after that 1991 Kentucky game.

We went to the dressing room first, and SEC Commissioner Kramer congratulated us. There were about a hundred 1991 SEC Football Champions hats available for the players; and after a few words and much clamor, we came back out.

A microphone was set up on the field. When it was my turn to speak I thanked everyone, and told them that the 1990 players deserved to have been in the Sugar Bowl and to be called champions. I told them that Kentucky had come to play; they outplayed us and outcoached us. But we had made enough big plays, the kind a champion must make at some point in a season.

Just about all 85,000 fans stayed, the music played and it was just a fantastic experience to watch and be part of as a Gator. I doubt if any of the players involved will ever forget that moment on the field, and neither will I.

ROAD TO THE CHAMPIONSHIP

GAME TEN

Florida 35, Kentucky 26
November 16, 1991, Ben Hill Griffin Stadium

GAINESVILLE, FLA. – Florida captured its first official SEC football championship in front of 84,109 spirited fans by holding off a determined bid from underdog Kentucky 35-26.

The Gators finished the conference season at 7-0, the first time in history a Florida team has posted an unbeaten, untied mark in league play, and the first time since 1977 that a conference school has won seven SEC games in a season.

Quarterback Shane Matthews set a league record with his 10th career 300-yard passing game, completing 26 of 39 passes for 362 yards and three touchdowns. The three TDs brought his season total to 27, also an SEC record.

He was also on the receiving end of a TD pass from wide receiver

FLORIDA 35, KENTUCKY 26

TEAM STATISTICS

	UK	UF
First Downs	24	29
Rushes-Yards	42-167	32-183
Passing Yards	236	381
Passes	20-33-0	27-40-3
Total Offense	403	564
Penalties/Yards	3-25	7-72
Fumbles-Lost	3-1	2-2
Possession Time	32:11	27:49

| Kentucky | 3 | 3 | 7 | 13 | – | 26 |
| Florida | 21 | 7 | 0 | 7 | – | 35 |

INDIVIDUAL LEADERS

Rushing: Kentucky – Jones 20-84 3TD, Walker 9-34, Rudolph 6-27; Florida – Rhett 26-154 1TD, McClendon 2-19, McNabb 3-15

Passing: Kentucky – Jones 17-29-216; Florida – Matthews 26-39-362 3 Int, 3TD, Sullivan 1-1-19 1TD

Receiving: Kentucky – Clark 8-101, Hobbs 2-35; Florida – Everett 3-108 2TD, W. Jackson 6-77, Houston 4-44, Rhett 5-35, Sullivan 3-44, Duncan 2-27, Matthews 1-19 1TD, Hill 1-8 1TD, McNabb 1-9

Alonzo Sullivan, a 19-yarder which gave him 29 touchdowns for which he is responsible, also a conference record.

Once again the Gator running game was built around sophomore Errict Rhett, who rushed for 154 yards and one touchdown, the ninth time in his career that he's rushed for more than 100 yards in a game – all nine coming against SEC foes.

Rhett reached the 1,000-yard mark for the season on his final play, a determined two-yard TD run with 2:22 remaining, accounting for the game's final score after Kentucky had closed a 28-3 deficit to 28-26 with just over seven minutes remaining.

Tre Everett, who had missed five straight games with a pulled hamstring, came back in style with three catches for 108 yards, two of which were sensational touchdown receptions.

Florida opened the game as though it would be a rout. Matthews hit Aubrey Hill on an eight-yard TD pass in the opening moments, then connected with Everett on a 65-yard catch-and-run bomb. He hit Everett again minutes later with a 33-yard scoring strike, and the Gators had 21 points in the first quarter.

Following Matthews' TD on the pass from Sullivan with 12:49 in the second quarter, the Wildcats shut down the Gator offense until the final clutch drive clinched the title for Florida. ■

18

SEC, FSU
BOTH IMPORTANT

We learned a painful lesson in 1990 that certainly changed our approach for 1991 and the coming seasons: Although the SEC is very important, so is FSU.

In 1990, the focus of our energy was directed almost totally toward finishing first in the conference. When we beat Kentucky and accomplished that, a euphoria set in among our team and coaches, and we all celebrated too much.

Winning the SEC wasn't just the top priority that year, it dominated our thinking from spring practice right through the season. We relaxed too much when that top goal was reached, and we couldn't get the edge back for the Seminoles.

We found out that as talented as FSU is, you had better be totally ready to play or you will be embarrassed like we were in Tallahassee in 1990. Coach Bobby Bowden and his staff always do a superb job, and for the Florida game they have their team at a fever pitch.

After losing up there, I found out I had inherited all those other losses in recent years. Some writers said I was just like all those other Florida coaches: I couldn't beat Bobby Bowden. We also began to understand that this game is important in the recruiting battles, because it is played right before recruiting starts for the next two months.

Prospects have told us that after that '90 game, FSU coaches told them, "We've kicked Florida's butts four straight years and we're going to kick them four more straight years. If you go to Florida, you're going to be a loser."

One of the six goals set at the end of spring practice was to beat FSU. Our players regarded this as a top priority for themselves and for our program. We didn't celebrate winning the championship in '91 for long, because we remembered what had happened the year before, and we had a game coming up that we desperately needed to win for ourselves and for all Gators.

FSU had been ranked number one all year, but came to our place ranked third after losing to Miami by one point, missing a short field goal at the end of the contest. Most Gator fans had rooted for FSU that day because they wanted them ranked first when they came to Florida Field. But it wasn't a big deal to us one way or the other. They were still a great football team, no less so because they lost by one point to the eventual national champion.

FSU was favored over us, the only time that had happened at home all year. Very seldom will we be the underdog in our own ballpark.

Not too much was said by our players in the week leading up to the game, in contrast to the year before, when one or two players just couldn't contain themselves and talked about how much they disliked FSU. This year I made a point of letting our players know that it never helps you to talk trashy about the other team. Only one or two of the FSU players said anything. We really didn't pay much attention to them; our players thought their remarks were comical.

Late in the fourth quarter of the game, in the torrid heat of Florida Field, an FSU offensive lineman who had made some trash-talk was throwing up on the field. Tony McCoy, our defensive tackle, shouted across at him: "If you'd been running instead of running your mouth, you wouldn't be getting sick out here."

It was hot that day. It was a noon kickoff for ABC-TV, and here it was 85 degrees on November 30. When we went out to warm up, it looked and sounded like all 85,000 fans were already in the stadium and on the edge of their seats.

That's about where they stayed. There was a lot of yelling and screaming from that point until the game was over. This was the most intense, emotional, electrifying game I have ever been involved with as a player or a coach at any level.

Some neutral people – sportswriters and even two officials – told me later that they had never seen a game where the fans wanted to win just as much as the players and coaches. It was so obvious that the game could be won or lost by either team on any single play that it kept everyone's emotions on razor's edge.

It was typical of so many big games in which both teams have outstanding offenses, but the defenses take over. This was a titanic defensive battle with absolutely vicious hitting. It is a testimony to the raw courage of both quarterbacks – our Shane Matthews and FSU's Casey Weldon – that they could finish the game. Both of them were pummeled by the opposing defense.

Early in the game, we had a touchdown called back for the first time all season. We had set it up beautifully with the hope of beating Terrell Buckley deep. He was FSU's All-American defensive back, the kind of player who gambles frequently; if he can step in and get an interception, he's going to go for it.

Shane dropped back and pumped, Tre Everett ran a little curl-and-go, and we threw about a 30-yard TD pass over Buckley, who bit hard on the fake. It was called back because Errict Rhett, the one back in the backfield, stepped over to block a linebacker and was in motion before the snap. On the next play Buckley stepped in and picked off a pass. He gambled twice, and a touchdown had been called back and he got an interception.

FSU also missed an almost certain touchdown early in the game when defensive end Darren Mickell made a huge play, one which most people didn't even remember after the game. They had second-and-goal at our one-yard line – actually they were about on the half-yard line. Darren made a sudden move of his head that made their offensive tackle and tight end jump, result-ing in an illegal procedure penalty to push them back to the six. From there they tried two passes, one of them incomplete; on the other, Harvey Thomas hit Weldon as he was trying to throw and the ball bounced back to the 28. They missed a field goal from there.

We went in at halftime with a 7-3 lead and it was quiet. I think everyone knew this game could turn on one play, and it would take tail-busting effort and concentration on every snap.

When we came back out, everybody was yelling. When FSU tried their war chant our crowd would just drown them out. When they did the tomahawk chop, our fans stopped it with the gator chomp. It was 75,000 of our people, 10,000 of their people and, obviously, our people were winning the noise battle.

In the third quarter, we had our best scramble play of the year. It was one of the few times Shane has ever scrambled out of the pocket to his right and had something good happen. When he started out of the pocket I thought: "Oh, no!" It was a crazy play. Harrison Houston ran a flat route and the outside receiver ran a curl. We were in a set with two tight ends and two wide receivers, and Charlie Dean, our added tight end, ran the wrong way.

That mistake helped set up the touchdown. Charlie ran a flat route also, so the free safety came out of the middle of the field to cover him. FSU was in an in-and-out man coverage with the line-backer covering man-to-man underneath. This left the line-backer on Harrison. They were standing there together as Shane scrambled out to his right with most of FSU's defense starting to react toward him.

Buckley was behind Willie Jackson, but headed toward Shane in an attempt to make a big play behind the line of scrimmage. He got there too late; the ball was already gone by that time. When Harrison saw Shane running, he ran up the sideline with Reggie Freeman, their linebacker, right with him. Fortunately, it was a little bit of an underthrow, which Harrison came back to catch on the FSU 42 as the linebacker stumbled and fell.

From there it was just a footrace, and because everyone was

out of position on defense, Harrison had a five-yard head start. With his speed, there was no way he would get caught, and Harrison sprinted into the end zone.

We were up 14-3, and the way our defense was playing that lead looked safe. We executed poorly on third-down conversions in the game, but finally we made a couple in the fourth quarter and got down to the FSU 13-yard line.

Willie ran a corner route. Shane had ample protection, but he had been rushed so hard most of the game that he let the pass go early, underthrowing Willie in the end zone and getting it picked off.

We really had a good chance to put the game away, but instead they came back and scored on a scrambled play. With Weldon trying to throw to a wide receiver coming across the field, Amp Lee, coming out of the backfield, intercepted the pass headed for an FSU teammate and scooted down the left sideline for a TD.

FSU, behind by five, called a timeout to get the play and proper personnel in the game for a two-point conversion. We were getting to that point in the game where timeouts can be a vital factor.

Their conversion play failed. We led 14-9 and had a chance to salt this away if only we could make a couple of first downs. Our fans probably jumped out of their seats when we came out throwing, but FSU had eight men up around the line of scrimmage, and I thought we had a chance to hit something big right then.

On third-and-10 Willie Jackson ran a short curl – he should have gone 11 yards, but he cut it back at seven. We came up just short, by about a yard and a half, at our 40 with just over two minutes remaining.

At that moment something flashed in my mind about what we had done one day when I coached the Tampa Bay Bandits. We were playing the Houston Gamblers in 1984 and had about the same situation. Houston ran their punt return team onto the field and then we ran our offense back out there. Houston called a timeout because they didn't want their punt return team attempting to defend us if we went for a first down.

So I called a timeout to explain to our team what we planned to do and also to make FSU think we were considering going for the first down. We first ran our punt team out there, so FSU ran their punt return team out onto the field. Just as our punt team was about to line up, suddenly they all ran off the field, and our offensive team ran on and lined up. There sat FSU with their punt return team and our offense on the field. Naturally, they called timeout to adjust their defense. We went ahead and punted, but it turned out to be a big play because we forced them to take a timeout. When the game got down to the final seconds, they were out of timeouts and couldn't stop the clock.

On FSU's final possession they moved down field until it was fourth-and-eight at our 12-yard line. Then a real scary play happened. Thank goodness I couldn't see it very well on the field and didn't clearly see what happened until I watched the videotape later, or my visor might have been hurled into the stands.

Weldon rolled out to his right. I was upset because we did not contain Weldon and he got to the outside, where their running back swung out and cut down defensive end Harvey Thomas. Our linebacker, Carlton Miles, didn't use the "scrape" technique properly to move down the line of scrimmage and wound up being blocked inside. Weldon had an enormous amount of time to find a receiver or run for the first down, or perhaps a touchdown. Luckily for the Gators, he elected to throw it back across the middle to a receiver cutting across, and free safety Will White got a hand on it.

We try to teach our defensive backs to knock the ball straight to the ground, but it hit Will's hand and bounced straight up in the air. I saw that happen and shouted to nobody in particular, "Well, who is going to get it next?"

Reviewing the tape the next day, I could see cornerback Del Speer watching FSU receiver Matt Frier come toward the ball with his hands in the air. I don't think Del ever saw the ball because he was chasing hard and didn't even see Will deflect the ball. If Del had seen the ball and gone for it, Matt probably would have been able to cut in front of him and catch it; fortunately,

Del hadn't and just decided to cut Frier down and eliminate him from the play.

I did what a coach almost always does when a big play is made: I looked to see if there were any flags on the field. When there weren't any, my pulse must have started moving back toward normal. When that ball hit the ground, the noise at Florida Field exceeded any noise ever before heard in that stadium. That's how I knew it wasn't caught.

We got the ball and ran three plays. On fourth down, I looked up and saw 24 seconds remaining on the clock. FSU was out of timeouts and couldn't stop it, and we didn't have to snap the ball.

The players and coaches on our sideline erupted with emotion at that moment, and the pressure of that physically and mentally taxing afternoon started to lift immediately. There was ultimate joy on one sideline, and ultimate despair on the other.

When the season was over we had the seniors out to my house for a steak and barbecued chicken cookout. I asked them what their favorite game was in 1991. This is something we started asking at Duke in 1987, and there were usually about five different answers, anywhere from North Carolina, N.C. State to Georgia Tech – one guy actually said Wake Forest one year. But that day, just about every Gator senior said FSU was our biggest win and their favorite game.

Brad Culpepper, who grew up in Tallahassee and had put up with a lot of stuff the past few years, obviously picked the FSU game. He even went so far as to say he could go home now without having to wear a cape and veil.

Offensive tackle Tony Rowell also picked FSU. I asked him, "Don't you understand the tradition of the SEC? Don't you see how big those wins were over Alabama – we had never beaten them in the state of Florida – and over Tennessee – who came in here ranked fourth in the nation?"

"Yes, Coach, those games were big," he answered, "but you haven't lived in Florida the last four years like we have."

Tony hit it right on the head, and I understand what he meant. Beating FSU was big, and we will never forget it.

ROAD TO THE CHAMPIONSHIP

GAME ELEVEN

Florida 14, FSU 9
November 30, 1991, Ben Hill Griffin Stadium

GAINESVILLE, FLA. – The largest crowd ever to watch a football game in the state of Florida – 85,461 – sat through stifling November heat to see the Gators win 14-9 in one of the all-time classics in the Florida-FSU series.

Florida's defense choked the touted Seminole offense for four quarters, and came up with a brilliant goal-line stand at the end to preserve the victory and give the Gators a school-record 10 wins in a season.

The emotional win was followed by a lengthy celebration at Ben Hill Griffin Stadium as Florida broke a four-game FSU winning streak in the series and extended its season winning streak to eight consecutive games.

The game, viewed by millions of people nationally on ABC-TV, pitted fifth-ranked Florida against third-ranked FSU, and the offenses were expected to dominate. Instead, it was a classic defensive struggle with the Gators holding the high-powered FSU offense to under 10 points for only the second time in the Seminoles' last 119 games. Florida's defense held the Seminole ground game, which was averaging more than 200 yards a game, to only 37 rushing yards.

Neither team scored in the first quarter, but FSU grabbed a 3-0 lead on a field goal with 8:31 left in the half. The Gators came back with their only sustained scoring drive of the day, a 10-play 76-yard march with Errict Rhett getting the TD on a three-yard run to make it 7-3 at halftime.

With 7:32 remaining in the third quarter Gator quarterback Shane Matthews was forced out of the pocket and found wide receiver Harrison Houston on a broken play which resulted in a 72-yard touchdown pass. The Gators held a 14-3 lead and had other

FLORIDA 14, FLORIDA STATE 9

TEAM STATISTICS

	FSU	UF
First Downs	20	16
Rushes-Yards	26-37	39-117
Passing Yards	305	208
Passes	24-51-1	13-30-3
Total Offense	342	325
Penalties/Yards	7-65	8-75
Fumbles-Lost	4-1	1-0
Possession Time	29:25	30:35

Florida State	0	3	0	6	–	9
Florida	0	7	7	0	–	14

INDIVIDUAL LEADERS

Rushing: FSU – Lee 9-24, Jackson 6-22, Bennett 5-19, Weldon 4-(-33); Florida – Rhett 24-109 1TD, McClendon 3-7, McNabb 3-5, Matthews 9-(-4)

Passing: FSU – Weldon 24-51-305 1 Int, 1TD; Florida – Matthews 13-30-208 3 Int,, 1TD

Receiving: FSU – K. McCorvey 6-89, Frier 6-61, Johnson 4-27, Lee 3-49 1TD; Florida – Houston 2-76 1TD, W. Jackson, 4-35, Rhett 4-31, Hill 1-41, McNabb 1-16 Everett 1-9

chances to pad the margin, but couldn't get into the end zone.

FSU scored on a 25-yard pass from Casey Weldon to Amp Lee with 5:24 remaining, cutting the deficit to 14-9, and then had it first-and-goal at Florida's nine-yard line before the Gator defense halted them with 2:11 left in the game.

It was a total team effort on defense, and ends Harvey Thomas and Darren Mickell were named the SEC Co-Defensive Players of the Week. They combined for 10 tackles, four pass breakups, two QB sacks, two caused fumbles and seven QB hurries on pass attempts. ∎

On January 1, 1992, we were in New Orleans' Louisiana Superdome playing Notre Dame in the Sugar Bowl, and although the final outcome was not what we all would like to have seen, the game was a memorable reward for our players for winning the SEC championship.

Our players had a good time, but they also worked hard at practice and concentrated on getting ready to play a very good opponent. I thought we played hard, but came up a little bit short because we failed to convert some good offensive opportunities into touchdowns in the first half and simply ran out of gas in the second half on defense.

We'll go into more detail on this game in a Q&A chapter later in the book that will explain my feelings about this game.

I want to make a point of saying the people who run the Sugar Bowl game did a first-class job of making our team feel welcome. The hospitality and game organization couldn't have been better, and we appreciate the time and energy they expended on our behalf.

THE SUGAR BOWL GAME

Notre Dame 39, Florida 28
January 1, 1992, Louisiana Superdome

NEW ORLEANS – Notre Dame overcame a nine-point deficit at halftime, and running back Jerome Bettis rushed for three touchdowns in the game's final five minutes against a banged-up Gator defense to lead the Irish to a 39-28 win in the 58th annual Sugar Bowl.

Playing without starting defensive end Harvey Thomas and All-SEC linebacker Tim Paulk, the Gators also lost the services of starting inside linebacker Carlton Miles to a back injury in the first quarter. The result: Notre Dame used an up-the-gut rushing attack in the second half that was responsible for 245 yards rushing in the game's final 30 minutes. The Irish rushed for just 34 yards in the first half.

SUGAR BOWL
NOTRE DAME 39, FLORIDA 28

TEAM STATISTICS

	UF	ND
First Downs	29	23
Rushes-Yards	33-141	49-279
Passing Yards	370	154
Passes	28-58-2	14-19-1
Total Offense	511	433
Penalties/Yards	4-40	3-15
Fumbles-Lost	0-0	4-3
Possession Time	31:00	29:00

Florida	10	6	0	12	– 28
Notre Dame	0	7	10	22	– 39

INDIVIDUAL LEADERS

Rushing: Florida – Rhett 15-63, McClendon 7-34, Matthews 7-27, McNabb 4-17; Notre Dame – Bettis 16-150 3TD, Culver 13-93, T. Brooks 13-68, Failla 1-(-2), Mirer 6 (-30)

Passing: Florida — Matthews 28-58-370 2 Int, 2TD; Notre Dame – Mirer 14-19-1-154 1 Int, 2TD

Receiving: Florida – W. Jackson 8-148 1TD, Houston 3-52 1TD, Sullivan 4-47, Hill 3-41, Rhett 4-38, McClendon 3-19, Everett 2-18, McNabb 1-7; Notre Dame – T. Smith 7-75 1TD, Dawson 2-49 1TD, Brown 1-11, Culver 1-6, Bettis 1-5, I. Smith 1-4, Pollard 1-4

To compound the problems of the injury-riddled defense, the Gator offense, which accumulated 511 yards in total offense, scored just two touchdowns after penetrating the Irish 20-yard line on seven occasions. Arden Czyzewski did convert on the opportunities by kicking a Sugar Bowl record five field goals on the night. The Gators' other scores came on a 15-yard pass from Shane

Matthews to Willie Jackson and a 34-yard pass from Shane to Harrison Houston late in the game.

Matthews, who was playing for the first time since having knee surgery in early December, had a record-setting night, completing 28 of 58 passes for 370 yards. The UF junior set five bowl records in all: most plays, 65 – 58 pass, 7 run; most yards gained, 397 – 370 passing, 27 rushing; most passing attempts, 58; most passing completions, 28; and most passing yards, 370.

Matthews' primary target of the night was wide receiver Willie Jackson. The sophomore finished the night with eight catches for 148 yards – both the second-highest bowl totals by a UF player in school history.

The Gators, who were making their first Sugar Bowl appearance since 1974 and the school's first as Southeastern Conference champions, got out of the gate early, jumping to a 10-0 lead in the first quarter. Florida had 10 first downs and gained 161 in total yards in the first quarter, while Notre Dame managed just one first down and 31 yards in total offense. The second quarter was still more of the same, and at halftime the Gators held a 16-7 advantage, had 10 more first downs than the Irish and almost double the total yardage of Notre Dame.

From there, however, Bettis and company took over. The 5-11, 247-pounder finished the night with 150 yards on 16 carries and three touchdowns. He was selected the Miller-Digby Memorial Award winner for his outstanding efforts. He scored on runs of three, 49 and 39 yards in the final 4:48 of the game to secure the Irish victory and prevent the Gators from winning their first Sugar Bowl in three trips to New Orleans. ∎

19

JERRI'S A STARR

Without a doubt one of the biggest reasons for any success I've had in coaching is my wife, Jerri. We were married September 14, 1966, just before my senior season at Florida, and she has been a strong influence and solid support since then.

We met as Florida students in 1964, my sophomore year. She had transferred from Greensboro (N.C.) Women's College.

Jerri is from Fort Lauderdale, one of three girls in the Starr family, all of whom were raised by their mother. Her father passed away when she was seven years old. She's the oldest daughter in the family, and basically she worked her way through college. She was always pretty prudent about finances, and still is to this day.

Jerri has a football background. Her great uncle was Rip Engle, the former Penn State head coach and one of the most outstanding coaches in the history of college football. The Starr family moved to Fort Lauderdale from the Pittsburgh area. She attended Fort Lauderdale Senior High, where she was a "Flying L."

That's the school's nickname.

She teaches aerobics classes to our football team, the swimming team, the volleyball team and the women's basketball and tennis teams. Most all of the teams at Florida have now asked her to teach during the off-season. Jerri loves being a part of something useful and positive like that.

I think that has been a big part of our team's success. She started teaching aerobics to our football team at Duke in 1989, and we won the ACC championship. She's taught aerobics at Florida to the 1990 and 1991 teams, which finished first both years; so rest assured we're going to keep having her do that.

Jerri is a family-oriented person. She thoroughly enjoys being around children, raising them and putting together family-type settings for us, and for our coaching staff. I've always felt coaching staffs need this to help everyone communicate and get along.

We have a very strong family atmosphere on our staff, and Jerri is one of the big reasons for this. I have been blessed there. I think every successful man must have a good wife and have things in order at home, and that has certainly been the case for me.

We have four children. Lisa, who is married now, and Amy are both graduates of Florida, and they are big sports fans. They come to all the games and certainly keep up with the teams I've coached through the years. They both jog and run; but as far as tennis or golf, those just aren't the types of activities either of them prefers.

Both of them were active members of Alpha Delta Pi sorority at Florida, as was their mother in the 1960s. Jerri is still active with the sorority's alumni group.

Our older son, Steve, is a sophomore wide receiver at Duke University, where he expects to graduate in about two years. He decided to go to school there and be a walk-on player, which was fine with me. He believes he has a good chance to play a lot of ball for them at wide receiver this season.

Steve was in the dressing room or serving as a ballboy at just about every game I coached from 1982 through 1989.

I remember when he was about 10 years old, he was a ballboy

in a USFL game we played against Pepper Rodgers and the Memphis Showboats. I told the Bandit players in the locker room before the game that we were going to try an onside kick on the opening kickoff.

Little Steve – our family calls him Bubba – was not very good at that age at keeping secrets. He went over to the Memphis sideline and spotted their quarterback, Mike Kelley, whom I coached at Georgia Tech. Steve told Mike they had better watch out for something on the opening kickoff.

Mike asked him if he meant there was going to be an onside kick, and Steve said he couldn't tell him that, but to watch out. So Mike told Pepper, who decided we wouldn't do something that crazy right away.

Sure enough, we tried the onside kick and recovered the ball, then went on to score a touchdown. After the game Pepper told the media they knew it was coming and still couldn't recover it. I told young Steve to keep his mouth shut on the sideline after that.

Steve loves football, and I think he likes the coaching aspect of it. It wouldn't surprise me if he wanted to be a coach one day.

Scotty is our youngest, and he certainly has been a joy for all of us. He's five years old and a smart little fellow. The other children have grown up into young adults, and it is wonderful to have a youngster like him to keep things hopping around the house.

My family has been healthy and God has blessed us, for which I am very thankful. Most of it goes back to Jerri, who is probably the closest thing to being a perfect coach's wife that exists.

JERRI SPURRIER:
Steve and I met in 1964. As an ADPi pledge, I was an Alpha Tau Omega 'Little Sister' and had as 'Little Brothers' Steve Spurrier and Steve Melnyk, who turned out to be one of the greatest golfers in Florida's history. That's where I really got to know Steve Spurrier. He finally asked me out on a date in January of 1965.

I immediately purchased a new dress for $42 at Donigan's in Gainesville; and when Steve picked me up he asked me why I was so dressed up, since we were only going to the drive-in movie. Most of our dates after that were spent cooking out with other athletes, friends and their dates, playing pinball machines, going to functions at the ATO house or across the street to parties at the Phi Delt house, where Steve's teammate, Charlie Casey, was a member.

We decided to get married in September of 1966, just before his senior football season. We were going to elope to Folkston, Georgia. Steve enlisted the help of a good friend, Fred Goldsmith, who is now the head football coach at Rice University. Fred went with us because he had just run away to Folkston to be married, and he could show us the way.

Well, we got lost and wound up in Kingsland, where we got married in a nice church. Steve gave me a $10 ring, and it's still the only wedding ring I wear. I've never had any desire to wear anything but my $10 ring.

We had to hustle on back to Gainesville because he had to go to practice, and I had a sorority rush meeting. Wasn't that romantic?

I was part of his senior year and have all the memories that he has. It's wonderful to have been part of that time in Gator history. Of all the people who have won the Heisman, only two were married during their senior year. I'm very lucky to have been part of that experience.

I wouldn't trade the life of being the wife of a football coach for anything. It's demanding and you must learn to adapt to a lot of situations, but it is rewarding.

20

SHANE MATTHEWS

I n December 1991, Shane Matthews was named Player of the Year in the Southeastern Conference for the second consecutive season. He entered the 1992 season rated as one of the prime candidates to win the Heisman Trophy.

His accomplishments as our quarterback the past two seasons have rewritten the record books, and he is very deserving of all the accolades bestowed upon him.

Many people say he is a product of our system. I don't believe it. Shane is our quarterback because he was able to do things better than anyone else. If it were the system, it wouldn't matter who you put out there. If you had a tryout camp, he might not look the prettiest, but he's going to make it happen for you in the game. He's the kind of player I love to coach.

I saw a quote from one of our players – I believe it was Brad Culpepper during the 1991 season – that said something like "you might have a great race car, but you still need an excellent driver to win, and Shane's our driver." Brad hit it on the head.

Shane has come further than any quarterback I have ever coached. I remember the first night of spring football practice in

1990 and my first look at him as one of our five scholarship quarterbacks.

After watching him at practice that night, I mentioned to John Reaves, who coaches our tight ends and works with the quarterbacks at times, that I didn't know if Shane would ever be able to play quarterback at Florida.

I told John that Shane didn't put much on the ball, and obviously we're going to throw it, and I didn't know if he could ever develop the arm strength and deliver enough velocity on it to be able to compete.

When I got the job in 1990 we inherited Kyle Morris, who basically had been the starting quarterback in 1989, along with Lex Smith, Donald Douglas, Brian Fox and Shane. Smith was a fairly highly recruited player who had played some. Fox had played on the scout team after transferring from Purdue where he played as a 1988 freshman. Douglas was a talented athlete with 4.4 speed in the 40-yard dash whose outstanding skills could have been better used at wide receiver or defensive back, in my opinion.

Matthews was virtually unknown. And he was so quiet you hardly knew he was out there on the field, although he worked very hard.

My job that spring was to coach all five and try to pick a quarterback that we would all have confidence in to lead our 1990 team to a big year. It was a good team I inherited from Galen Hall and his staff, but one of these quarterbacks would have to be the key if we were to have an outstanding season.

When we started spring drills, Shane was number five on the depth chart, basically because the others had more experience – all four of them had started at least one college game. Also, he probably belonged there because he had the weakest arm.

Shane might have gotten in for three or four plays in the first scrimmage, not much at all, but we hoped to alternate all five guys in the big scrimmage at the end of two weeks of practice. We did try to do that, which is difficult with so many at the position.

After practice I was walking off the field, and Bo Bayer, who worked in our athletic dorm administration, introduced me to

Bill Matthews, Shane's father.

Bill, the head football coach at Pascagoula High School in Mississippi, had driven a long way to watch his son play in the scrimmage, and Shane didn't even get a snap. Shane's uniform was still completely clean, and he had already left the field and gone to the locker room.

It didn't dawn on me that Shane hadn't played until I met his father. I told Bill it was my fault his son didn't play and that it's difficult to practice five quarterbacks. He told me that as a coach he understood and wasn't upset, then added: "I just want to tell you one thing. Shane wants a chance to be your number one quarterback; he thinks he can play as well as any of your QBs here, and he wants that shot."

That was the first time I had heard that Shane really wanted to play. Most quarterbacks are vocal, and most of them believe they are better than they really are, to tell you the truth. Shane is so quiet and laid-back, a young man who is content to go out and do well on the practice field.

But he never said, "Hey, I want to be the number one quarterback, and I think I'm good enough." I mean, he never said it in word or action.

When his dad told me that, I guess I developed a little more interest in Shane and thought we should give him more of an opportunity. So although he was still fifth team, he did start alternating more with the others.

The next week two things happened. Donald Douglas, whom I had talked with seriously about the possibility of his switching to wide receiver or defensive back, decided to transfer. He was struggling in our system of dropping back, making choices and throwing the ball. I had coached Donald as hard as I could those first three weeks and, in my opinion, he could help the team and himself more at another position.

But Donald wanted to play quarterback and felt he should go back home to Houston to be closer to his mother. So he transferred to the University of Houston.

Then Brian Fox broke a bone in his foot and was out the last week or so, seven or eight practices in all. This left us with only three scholarship quarterbacks.

Shane then started getting in a lot in the scrimmages, operating generally with the second or third team against the first defense. When he got into the scrimmages, I noticed that all of a sudden his footwork was a little quicker than it was when he was just practicing against the air; his ball had more velocity and got to the receiver quicker in the scrimmage than it did in practice.

And, the most pleasant surprise of all, his funky little throwing motion disappeared when guys were chasing him and he had to throw the ball quickly.

So, Shane caught my eye and the eyes of the other coaches and the players. We started thinking that maybe this guy could play after all. I remember our talented little wide receiver Terence Barber coming back to the huddle one time and saying, "I didn't use to think so, but you might be a player."

Slowly but surely it became obvious that Shane was indeed a player.

The best thing about Shane at that point was that he could get the snap from center. It seems like all the other quarterbacks dropped about one out of every eight or nine in just the center-quarterback exchange. Shane could hand the ball off to the running back and get it right in the belly where it belonged, and that was encouraging for a coach to watch.

At the end of spring drills, we went to Jacksonville to play the Orange and Blue Game in the Gator Bowl because natural grass was being installed on our playing field in Gainesville.

I put Morris and some of the walk-on quarterbacks on one team, and Matthews and Smith on the other one. Coach Reaves was coaching Shane and Lex on the Orange team, and right before we went over to Jacksonville he asked me if he could start Shane.

We wanted both of them to play an equal amount of time, but Shane started and had a marvelous game. He completed nine of 15 pass attempts for 146 yards and three touchdowns with no interceptions in about two quarters of action.

In the meantime, Kyle really struggled with the Blue team. He threw some balls that really made me nervous, lobbing a few of them down the middle to the free safety and winding up with four interceptions. I kept thinking, what if that were the Georgia Bulldogs out there on the other side.

Shane's team won, and he clearly deserved the MVP award he won that day. Suddenly, the race for the first-team quarterback position was wide open. I told the players that probably the guy who has the best summer of working on his mechanics of throwing and on his footwork, and comes back in the best physical and mental shape, would be the starting quarterback.

We started fall practice alternating Kyle and Shane and working Brian in some. It soon became evident the battle was between Kyle and Shane, who were and still are the best of friends.

A week before the opening game against Oklahoma State, I announced that Shane was our starter. I thought it was important that our team knew he was our quarterback, that he had the first opportunity to see if he could carry the burden of starting.

Shane had said about a week earlier that he thought I would pick Kyle because he was more experienced and had played in some big games for Florida. I picked the person I thought could lead us to a championship, and the player who in the long run would be the best for the Gator football team.

In late July of that year I had predicted to the Jacksonville Gator Club that whoever our quarterback was, he would be the All-SEC quarterback that season. Shane, who was at the back of the room along with Kyle at that meeting, made me look like a prophet.

In the first game of the season against Oklahoma State, Shane hit three straight passes of 18 to 25 yards on our first possession, and we scored in about a minute and a half. He had a wonderful debut.

The next week there were a few moments in the first half against Alabama when I thought about replacing him, but I went back to my original feeling that he was going to be our best player and we needed to stick with him.

If there ever was a good decision it was that one, because

Shane was able to bring us back in the second half, making some marvelous throws. We were able to come from 10 points behind to win at Alabama, which proved to be maybe the most important game we've won in the past two seasons.

The coaching process that started in the spring with Shane began with our changing his throwing motion a little bit. He somehow had been taught that you needed to stick the ball way up in the air and throw it completely overhand. His elbow was so high that it messed up his shoulder rotation.

I believe that throwing the football is a very natural motion, and that a three-quarters overhand delivery, the same way a baseball pitcher throws a fastball, is best.

We taught Shane not to stick the ball up in the air so much and to use more of a normal throwing motion, while using his legs to transfer his weight properly.

During the 1990 season he made remarkable progress in the mechanics of throwing. By the end of the year he was often overthrowing Ernie Mills and Tre Everett – a pair of extremely fast receivers – on the deep ball. The ball was coming out like a bullet.

I remember a couple of times the players looked back and asked, "Did Shane throw that one?" He was throwing perfect spirals like frozen ropes down the field. That was because he had improved his mechanics.

Shane makes our system work because he has the ability to make decisions under pressure. Playing QB in our system is probably 75 percent to 80 percent mental.

There are just so many decisions for the quarterback to make under pressure, and Shane really picked up our system quickly and made it work. In the past two years he has not had what I call a stupid interception. He's had some interceptions, which all quarterbacks have, but just about 90 percent of his interceptions are on balls thrown downfield, and we are a down-the-field passing team.

We're not a sort-of-throw-it-around-the-line-of-scrimmage passing team. We are going to throw the ball down the field, and that's why we are able to average around 300 yards or more passing each game, each season.

One of the nicest things about coaching Shane is his dad's a coach also, and a highly respected state championship coach at that.

Early in the 1990 season, when Shane would run out of the pocket too quickly or choose the wrong side or the wrong receiver, I would sort of jump on him when he came off the field and say, "Shane, we can't win if you're not going to throw it to who you're supposed to or if you're going to keep running out of the pocket when we've got them picked up."

Basically, what I was trying to do was to get him to concentrate on the play, on the game, and get him to thinking about what was going on out there. Some people have trouble accepting criticism from their coaches, but not Shane; it just bounces off him.

I remember one Sunday afternoon as the team was meeting, I told Shane that I was sorry for yelling at him a little too strongly in the first quarter of the game the day before.

He said, "Coach, don't worry about it. My dad has yelled at me a lot worse than you ever have." Right then I knew that it didn't bother his play and that he knew his coach was just trying to get his attention on carrying out his quarterback assignment as best he could.

A lot of times you'll see our coaches, myself included, trying to get the players' attention early in the game. Very seldom will you see us do much yelling at all in the second half of a game. Early in a game we're trying to get the concentration level up to its maximum point, so coaches are trying to get their attention. But each time we yell at them, hopefully, you'll see us pat them on the back to try to get them back up.

One thing I like to stress to them when they make mistakes is they are too good to be playing like they are. I've told Shane that several times when he makes the bad throws, chooses the wrong side or runs out of the pocket too quickly. I'll say, "Shane, you're too good a quarterback to start acting like a mediocre player."

When we yell at players on the sideline we're not calling them names; we are attempting to get their total, undivided attention. Shane accepts this as well as any quarterback I've ever coached.

We have, I think, just a wonderful player-coach relationship, and I don't believe you could ask for a higher-quality person to work with than Shane Matthews.

He has had so many brilliant games, made so many courageous throws under extreme physical pressure, that perhaps he is sometimes taken for granted. In my mind, what he has accomplished in leading us to two first-place SEC finishes in his two years as quarterback makes him the best quarterback in Gator history. No other quarterback has done what he has done as a Gator.

It also justifies him as a leading Heisman Trophy candidate for 1992. If he and our team can continue to perform at a peak level he certainly could win it, and would deserve to do so. I know he isn't concerned about individual records because he is a team player in every sense of the word, but it's something his teammates would very much like to see him achieve.

I'm no expert on what it takes for a player to win the Heisman Trophy. I do know that in this day and time a school doesn't have to go to extremes to hype a player for this award. There is so much exposure on TV and in the print media that the voters across the country should receive ample opportunity to fairly judge everyone.

We'll let Shane's record speak for itself. We are 19-4 overall and 13-1 in the SEC with him as our quarterback, and we've been the top team in our league both years.

He has set six SEC records and 21 school records, and is close to breaking many more in 1992. Probably the most remarkable school record he has broken is passing for more than 300 yards in 10 games. To put this in perspective, in the 83 years of Gator football before Shane Matthews, there were only 11 games in which Florida passed for more than 300 yards.

He's one of only five players in conference history to be named the player of the year twice, and only Heisman Trophy winner Herschel Walker of Georgia has won it three times.

All of this is a good foundation for Shane going into 1992. Now we'll all have to go out and play and see what happens.

SHANE MATTHEWS' RECORD BOOK

SEC career records (1)
■ 300-yard passing games (10)

SEC single-season records (4)
■ Touchdown passes (28, 1991)
■ Touchdowns responsible for (30 – 28 passing, 1 rushing, 1 receiving, 1991)
　■ Total offense (3,140 – 3,130 passing, 10 rushing, 1991)
　■ Completion percentage (60.6 percent, 1990, min. 200)

SEC single-game records (1)
■ Touchdown passes (5, 1991)

UF career records (2)
■ 300-yard passing games (10)
■ Consecutive 200-yard passing games (16, current)

UF single-season records (15)
■ Touchdown passes (28, 1991)
■ Yards passing (3,130, 1991)
■ Touchdowns responsible for (30 – 28 passing, 1 rushing, 1 receiving, 1991)
　■ Total offense (3,140 – 3,130 passing, 10 rushing, 1991)
　■ Consecutive 200-yard passing games (11, 1991)
　■ Touchdown passes by a junior (28, 1991)
　■ Yards passing by a junior (3,130, 1991)
　■ Total offense by a junior (3,140 – 3,130 passing, 10 rushing, 1991)
　　■ 300-yard passing games (5, 1990 and 1991)
　　■ 200-yard passing games (11, 1991)

- Consecutive 300-yard passing games (3, 1990)
- Yards passing by a sophomore (2,952, 1990)
- Total offense by a sophomore (2,925 – 2,952 passing, 27 rushing, 1990)
- Total plays (450, 1990)
- Completions (229, 1990)

UF single-game records (4)
- Passing yards by a junior (362, 1991)
- Touchdown passes (28, 1991)
- Total offense (377 – 351 passing, 26 rushing, 1990)
- Total offense by a sophomore (377 – 351 passing, 26 rushing, 1990)

21

Q & A

I get a wide range of questions in the mail from interested Gators around the state and across the country. Here are a few of the more interesting queries, with my responses:

Why do you throw your visor?

My actions and responsibilities on the sideline are probably different from those of most head coaches, and this perhaps is why I get so emotionally involved in the game. First of all, as head coach I must make the decisions on team strategy during the course of a game. That's my responsibility, but it doesn't take a lot of time on the sideline or in pregame thinking. They're pretty much common-sense decisions.

Unlike most head coaches, I also act as offensive coordinator on the sideline. To me, the reason we have been so successful on offense and in throwing the ball is that we're striving for perfection.

Dr. Sydney Harris, in an article titled "Fierce Competitors," wrote, "They're not really people who love to win, but rather they are people who are always striving for perfection."

When we coach our offense, we aren't just trying to win, we're trying to play the perfect game. We want to go up and down the field and score a touchdown every time we touch the ball.

When I see players – quarterbacks, receivers, linemen, whoever – not playing up to potential, that is upsetting to me. When I see that a receiver didn't run a good route or didn't come out of his break correctly, or I see that the quarterback didn't make the throw he is capable of making, then it's frustrating to me.

It's frustrating not so much because of the score of the game, but because we're trying to get our players to play as close to perfect as possible. We realize we're not going to reach perfection, but I believe that if the players sense the coaches are upset, then they will want to do something about it. If the coaches' attitude is "that's not bad, that's OK, we're going to miss a few," then the players will accept bad plays as just part of the game.

Bad plays will happen, of course, but we need to show displeasure when they occur.

So, when it comes to my throwing the visor – well, some coaches can mask their emotions, but I'm just not one of them.

Why do you close Gator Club meetings by singing "We Are the Boys of Old Florida"?

First of all, it's a lot better than just saying "goodbye, we'll see you next year." It's fun to sing. It gets people up and excited, and that's the positive note the crowd leaves on that evening.

More importantly, I think the singing of that song between the third and fourth quarters is a wonderful tradition at home games, and the words have real meaning for our people.

I particularly like the ending: "In all kinds of weather, we'll all stick together for F-L-O-R-I-D-A." It's a great reminder that we are all part of the University of Florida, and our loyalty is what makes it such an outstanding school. When we are all on the same team, and we put ourselves into living the words of that song, the Gators are going to be tough to beat.

What is your opinion of Emmitt Smith?

I have a lot of respect for Emmitt as a person, not just as a football player. He is a young man who has character, pride and determination to succeed.

I think any young man who has a chance to make himself and his family financially secure by leaving school early and turning professional should do that, if he is positive he can succeed at that level. This was the choice Emmitt made, and it was the correct one for him and his family.

Since that time, he obviously has been very successful in professional football, and he has remained a strong, loyal Gator who attends every game he can possibly make. It was great to see him after the win over FSU in 1991 proudly running around the field waving a Gator banner.

If it were still legal to have former players participate in recruiting, Emmitt would be the first person we would ask to help. I think it shows a lot about his character that he was back in school last spring, working on getting his degree from the university.

What about coaching in the NFL?

My commitment was made in 1989, when I decided to accept the offer to coach at Florida. There were other opportunities for me maybe to enter the NFL as a head coach, and it was necessary to determine what the best alternative was for me and my family.

My choice was to come to Florida, and I think this is the best job in coaching. The powers-that-be would have to run me out of the position for me to leave.

We have everything it takes to be successful at Florida. It's one of the finest academic institutions in the country, and the athletic program is among the five best in the country each year. We won the SEC's All-Sports championship for 1991-92 in men's and women's sports – the first time that has ever been accomplished in our conference. We have outstanding facilities and financial support, and we recruit in the state of Florida, perhaps the best high school football state in the nation.

What happened in the Sugar Bowl?

There were a few people upset about the loss, but none of

them said they would be willing to swap a victory in the Sugar Bowl for the FSU win, or for a win against Alabama or Tennessee or Auburn or Georgia.

Looking back, beating those teams that have been beating the Gators for so many years is what's most important about the 1991 season. Given a choice, you would want to win your conference games and games against your traditional rivals.

That Gator team did things that had never been done before. They got to the Sugar Bowl, but we weren't quite at the level to be able to win it that time.

We had hoped Miami would be in the game, but it didn't work out. All of us have to do what is best for our school. For them, staying at home making an extra million dollars and having a better chance to win the national championship was probably in their best interest.

Our dreams of playing for the national championship in the Sugar Bowl were very, very remote. We played Notre Dame, which had three losses and was ranked 17th. We would have had to hope that Washington would barely lose to Michigan, and that somehow Nebraska would beat Miami to have had a chance at winning the national championship.

Our goal was to win the Sugar Bowl, but the trip was also a reward for our players. We let them have a good time for the first three days, then we got serious and prepared to play the game.

I think we were ready to play. We came out playing very well, but some things happened that didn't go our way: We got field goals instead of TDs, and then had a few injuries on defense.

We just didn't have the staying power in the second half to hold off a very physical Notre Dame team and sustain a victory. I thought Notre Dame played extremely well. Once their offense got in gear, we just couldn't stop their big fullback Jerome Bettis. Rick Mirer, their quarterback, had an outstanding night.

What about recruiting and the future?

During my first recruiting season, in early 1990, we were under the threat of sanctions from an NCAA investigation of alleged violations in the mid-1980s. We signed some good players, but the class was certainly not a Top 10 group.

The next year, after the no-bowl sanction had been carried out, and we had finished at 9-2, we signed a lot more good players; it was a Top 10 class this time. We were starting to gain some ground.

The third year we won 10 games, finished 7-0 in the SEC and won the conference championship, and we had an outstanding group of recruits. *SuperPrep Magazine* rated our class number one in the nation, and most recruiting experts ranked us in the Top 5. What this means is we are attracting quality players; if we continue to recruit as we should, the future should be bright for the Gators.

We can consistently have a Top 5 class, mainly because:

■ We have exceptional high school talent in our state.

■ Florida is the oldest and highest-rated academic institution in our state, and the top-ranked state university in the SEC.

■ We have the largest stadium in the state of Florida, and our fans' support – 84,000 to 85,000 at each home game – is excellent. Opponents say Ben Hill Griffin Stadium is the toughest place to play in our conference.

■ There is solid alumni support through contributions to the program. We are financially better off than most of the schools we compete against.

How is your relationship with athletic director Jeremy Foley?

We have a dynamic young athletic director in Jeremy Foley. I believe he will prove to be one of the best in the nation in leading the way for our program over the next few years.

He is very enthusiastic and positive – a lot like me in that he sees the advantages at the University of Florida, unlike some people in the past who have dwelled on negatives.

Jeremy is very easy to work with as my boss. I'm confident he'll do what is right for our football program and will support us. Florida's goals are high for all programs, and he will set the direction for the Gators.

What is your attraction to the game of golf?

First, it's the toughest sport anyone could ever attempt to play. It is you against the course, and nobody else can carry the load for you if you have a poor day. It requires competitive spirit, concentration, patience and decision-making.

Golf is fascinating. All of us think we should play better than we do. We think "this is the day I will really play well" and then go out and hit just enough good shots to bring us back the next day.

When you really mess up you must come back. The person who can forget that bad shot and try again will be the winner most of the time.

Golf relates to life. The ball is not always going to bounce your way, and the putts are not always going to drop. You have to just keep rolling the putts toward the hole and eventually some or all of them will start going in. The true grinder who competes the hardest generally will be the winner.

It also relates to football. The team that doesn't let bad breaks discourage it and just keeps grinding away – trying their hardest – will eventually win most games.

From the standpoint of personal satisfaction, playing the game in the off-season, I prefer to play courses from the back tees, play the ball down in the fairway in medal play competition and count all the shots, even those little six-inch putts.

My golf game is mostly intense and serious during the off-season. However, when football practice starts, I put the clubs away and don't give the game much thought until the season and recruiting are over.

That's probably a lot different from the impression of those who believed the rumor that I was a "country club coach." I remember one morning I was in the office at 5:30 a.m., and one of my assistants told me I had better not let anyone know I came in that early or it would ruin my reputation.

What about the TV video on the Bandits that contained foul language?

The USFL wanted to do a documentary on a season in the life of one of their teams. Our owner, John Bassett, thought it was worthwhile, and told all of us to cooperate. We were given assurances that we could review the tape and remove objectionable material.

This was for the 1985 season. The photographers and sound men were allowed to go everywhere: private parties, team meetings, the locker room, the sidelines and anywhere else they wanted.

Football is an emotional, physical game. It is highly competitive. When you have these factors involved there is going to be language used that wouldn't be used in the normal day-to-day activities we all pursue.

Two tragic events took place. Mr. Bassett became ill and passed away, and the USFL folded after that season. Somehow, the enormous amount of videotape never got reviewed or approved. It then showed up years later as a commercial product.

The first time I saw the documentary was at a reunion for the Bandits in Tampa after I had returned to Florida. Then it started showing up on television.

Needless to say, I was shocked and not real happy about the unedited version being made public.

ABOUT THE AUTHORS

STEVE SPURRIER

Steve Spurrier's first pass attempt in his career at Florida came against Southern Methodist University in the 1964 season-opener. It resulted in a 56-yard completion to Jack Harper to set up the game's first score. Three years later, in 1966, his final throw was a 17-yard completion to Larry Smith against Miami at Florida Field.

In between, Spurrier became the most celebrated athlete in the history of the university, winning the 1966 Heisman Trophy and leading the Gator football team to heights never before reached. He had come to Florida from Johnson City, Tennessee, rated as one of the top recruits ever attracted by Florida, and he delivered on that potential.

In three seasons at quarterback, he broke every school record for game, season and career in both passing and total offense, and he cracked all the SEC passing standards. This performance earned him All-American honors in 1965 and 1966, and he was named conference player of the year in '66.

In the Sugar Bowl game after the 1965 season, Spurrier broke six passing and total-offense records for the bowl. He is still the only player from a losing team ever to be named Most Valuable Player in that bowl classic.

The Gator career statistical chart shows him with 392 completions in 692 attempts, good for 4,848 yards and 36 touchdowns, all record accomplishments. He had 5,290 total offense yards during his career. In 1965 alone he gained 2,213 yards, 317 of which were against Auburn – new standards for the Gators at that time. His 27 completions against Auburn in 1966 stood as a Florida record until Wayne Peace posted 28 against FSU in 1982.

Still, statistics alone don't tell the story of what he did for Gator football. Spurrier and his teammates in the mid-1960s took a program that had never won the conference title and had no major bowl appearances to its credit, and put it on the national gridiron map.

Florida's wide-open passing style was ahead of its time in college football. Spurrier directed an attack that resulted in nine second-half comeback wins, eight of them in the fourth quarter. His skill and confidence under pressure astounded opponents, fans and the media.

It all started with that opening game against SMU at Florida Field in September of 1964. The Gators were struggling on offense and the game was scoreless when Spurrier entered his first collegiate game in the second quarter. On his first series, it was third-and-nine at Florida's 37-yard line when Spurrier found Harper and made the 56-yard completion of his first pass attempt. Harper carried the ball to SMU's seven-yard line, and Florida scored two plays later. Spurrier's first touchdown pass, a 10-yarder to Charlie Casey, came in the fourth quarter to seal the victory.

The following week, in raucous Memorial Stadium in Jackson, Mississippi, Florida trailed host Mississippi State in the fourth quarter, and the cowbells were ringing. Spurrier calmly guided the Gators to within range of a 33-yard field goal by Bob Lyle, which tied the score at 13-13.

Florida later took over the ball with 27 seconds remaining, and Spurrier hit Casey with three consecutive sideline passes.

Lyle's 41-yard field goal with one second left won the game 16-13, and the Spurrier legend for comebacks began.

The following week at Florida Field, Ole Miss, the preseason choice to win the SEC title, came to town ranked in the Top 10 in the nation. They left town a badly beaten team as Spurrier connected with Casey for TD passes of 43 and 19 yards in a 30-14 Gator victory.

In the final game of 1964, the Gators trailed Miami 10-0 in the fourth quarter when Spurrier entered the contest in relief of starter Tom Shannon and guided Florida to a pair of TDs and a 12-10 victory. He was named SEC Sophomore of the Year the following week.

Florida went to its first major bowl after the 1965 season, facing Missouri in the Sugar Bowl on January 1, 1966. Spurrier was named first team All-American after leading the Gators to a 7-3 record. In the process, he set 18 school records and six SEC records for game, season or career.

During the 1965 season, he completed 175 of 332 pass attempts for 2,245 yards and 16 touchdowns, while rushing for another 222 yards to bring his total offense to 2,467 yards, all school marks at the time. Since the SEC's inception in 1933, no junior had posted numbers of that magnitude.

Two regular-season games in 1965, against Georgia and FSU, are still etched in the memories of Gator fans. They are classic Spurrier miracles.

Florida trailed the Bulldogs 10-7 in a typically tense, physical battle in Jacksonville, Florida. With just under four minutes remaining, the Gators got the ball at their own 22-yard line, and in two plays got the winning touchdown. Spurrier hit Casey first for 42 yards, then Harper for 36 yards and the score, which made the final margin 14-10. It was a stunning defeat for the Bulldogs, who had appeared to have the game under control.

The victory over FSU in the season's final game was even more dramatic. No Seminole team had ever beaten Florida in Gainesville, but FSU was leading 17-16 after scoring a touchdown with 2:10 remaining in the game.

"We didn't know what to come up with on the sideline while FSU was getting ready to kick off," recalls Ray Graves, Florida's head coach at that time. "Then Steve came over, put his arm around me and calmly told me not to worry, that we were going to score and win."

Spurrier was just as calm on the field as he took Florida 71 yards on six plays in only 58 seconds, scoring the winning touchdown on a 25-yard pass to Casey. He hit four passes on the drive and ran once for a first down. Allen Trammell returned an interception 30 yards for a TD with seconds remaining, to make the final score 30-17.

Florida's Sugar Bowl appearance was a nightmare. With just over 10 minutes left in the game, Missouri led 20-0, totally dominating the contest. Then Spurrier took the Gators on three scoring drives, throwing TD passes to Casey and Harper and running for another score.

But the Gators chose to go for two points after every touchdown, and wound up losing 20-18. Despite the loss, Spurrier was named the game's MVP. He broke six bowl records, some of which remained intact until Shane Matthews broke them in the Gators' 1992 Sugar Bowl game against Notre Dame.

In 1966, Spurrier became the first Gator player to adorn the covers of the preseason football publications. He and Purdue's Bob Griese were the favorites to capture the Heisman Trophy. When it was all over, Spurrier not only won the Heisman, but he captured it by the largest margin in the history of balloting for this premier honor in college football.

He had led Florida to a 9-2 record, brought the Gators from behind for wins against FSU, North Carolina State and Auburn, set several more school and conference records and helped propel his team into the Orange Bowl game against Georgia Tech.

It was the Auburn game of that 1966 season that brought him everlasting fame. Florida was 6-0 entering the game and ranked seventh in the nation. Heisman Trophy ballots had gone out that week and were due back the week after the game. The press box was full of media representatives from as far away as New York.

Despite one of the most outstanding performances of Spurrier's college career, the Gators were tied at 27-all with the Tigers, and only 2:12 remained in the game. Spurrier had already completed an SEC-record 27 passes for 259 yards and one touchdown. He had also punted five times, for an average of 47.4 yards a kick, to keep Auburn's offense at bay.

Spurrier had taken Florida from its own territory to the Auburn 24-yard line, but the Gators faced fourth-and-14 for a first down. The 40-yard field goal attempt was out of the range of Florida's regular kicker, Wayne Barfield. Coach Graves called a timeout, and Spurrier said he could make the kick. The rest is history that will live forever in Gator hearts and minds: Spurrier calmly booted a game-winning 40-yard field goal for a 30-27 victory.

A record crowd of 60,511 filled Florida Field that day. Today, if you listen to the tales told by fans who said they witnessed that kick, you would think that attendance had been over 100,000. Such is the impact left on Florida football by the career of its most famous player.

NORM CARLSON

Norm Carlson joined the Gator athletic staff as sports information director in 1963, the same year Steve Spurrier started his freshman year at Florida.

Carlson now serves as assistant athletic director. He coordinates the Gators' media relations program, serves as Coach Spurrier's administrative assistant, writes football articles for game programs and other publications, and is the athletic department historian and senior advisor.

Following graduation from the University of Florida in 1956, he was a sportswriter for the *Atlanta Journal* until 1959 and then was sports information director at Auburn University from 1959 through 1963. He served eight years on the NCAA public relations committee, 10 years as executive secretary of the Florida

Sportswriters Association, eight years on the board of directors of the Football Writers Association and six years as color announcer on the Florida radio football network.

Carlson is a member of the College Sports Information Directors Hall of Fame and the Citrus Bowl Hall of Fame, and he is secretary of the Florida Sports Hall of Fame Foundation.

He has been president of the SEC publicity directors five different times.

His relationship with Steve Spurrier goes back 30 years, and for much of this period he has served as advisor, close friend and confidant to the Florida head football coach.

Carlson is a native of St. Louis, Missouri. His wife's name is Sylvia, and he has eight children and three grandchildren.

INDEX

A

ACC, 3, 13, 22, 29, 32, 34, 69, 78, 173

Akron, University of, 52

Alabama, University of, 32, 38, 39, 40, 42, 43, 44, 49, 52, 55, 69, 72, 85, 90, 93-101, 104, 108, 150, 165, 179, 180, 188

All-America(n), 30, 75, 81, 146, 151, 193, 195

Allen, George, 30

Alvarez, Carlos, 80

American Association of Universities (AAU), 12

Anderson, Gary, 77

Anderson, Jerry "Red", 63, 75, 76, 137

Anderson, Myrick, 107, 109

Arena Football League, 73, 79

Arnsparger, Bill, 13, 14, 15, 84, 123, 124

Attila the Hun, 47

Auburn University, 4, 38, 48, 51, 52, 53, 54, 55, 56, 57, 60, 61, 62, 65, 69, 75, 85, 128, 134-140, 188, 194, 196, 197

B

Bailey, Charlie, 31

Bandits, Tampa Bay, 2, 13, 18, 25, 29, 30, 31, 76, 77, 78, 80, 136, 163, 173, 191,

Barber, Terence, 41, 63, 178

Barfield, Wayne, 197

Barnhart, Tony, 94

Bartley, Fee, 85, 134

Bassett, John, 29, 30, 31, 191

Bates, Jim, 41, 45, 46, 73, 76

Bayer, Bo, 176

Becksvoort, John, 129

Bengals, Cincinnati, 30

Bennett, Ben, 19, 20, 21, 27, 28

Bestwick, Dick, 27

Bettis, Jerome, 168, 170, 188

Biskup, John, 111

Blunk, Joel, 28

Bolt, Wayne, 54

Boone, Greg, 28

Bowden, Bobby, 70, 159

Brandon, Mike, 85, 105, 128

Breakers, Boston, 30

Brown, Chris, 34

Brown, David, 21, 22

Browns, Cleveland, 73
Bryan, Robert, Dr., 13, 14, 15
Bryant, Paul (Bear), 40
Buccaneers, Tampa Bay, 31, 79, 81
Buckley, Terrell, 161, 162
Burnett, Bryce, 90
Burns, Jack, 31
Butters, Tom, 11, 27, 32

C

Cain, Harry, 142
Cardinals, Phoenix, 11, 34
Carlson, Norm, 72, 143, 197
Carter, Dale, 47
Carter, Kevin, 128
Casey, Charlie, 174, 194, 195, 196
Casey, Herbert, 140
Cassisi, Nick, Dr., 13, 15, 135
Castor, Chris, 28
Chandler, Wes, 147
Chiles, Lawton, 66
Clemson University, 3, 25, 27, 32, 33, 34, 54, 78
Collins, Geri, 74
Collins, Jim, 33, 74
Coolidge, Calvin, President, 3
Cowboys, Dallas, 124
Culpepper, Brad, 8, 75, 85, 86, 87, 88, 90, 97, 99, 101, 116, 120, 131, 134, 151, 165, 175
Curry, Bill, 65, 66, 137, 149
Cuthbert, Randy, 22, 34, 77
Czyzewski, Arden, 42, 56, 90-

91, 97, 100, 105, 116-117, 120, 139, 169

D

Daniels, Dexter, 81
DarDar, Kirby, 105, 109
Davis, Antoine, 45, 46
Davis, Dexter, 34
Davis, Mouse, 73
Dawsey, Lawrence, 70
Dean, Charlie, 162
Dean, Terry, 134
Dickey, Doug, 25, 26, 80, 123, 124
Dilweg, Anthony, 21, 22
Dixon, Cal, 85, 86, 87
Dixon, Dwayne, 78-79, 136
Dizney, Don, 29
Donahue, Ken, 73
Dooley, Vince, 61, 104, 142, 143
Dotsch, Rollie, 30, 78
Douglas, Donald, 176, 177
Drive, Detroit, 73
Duke University, 3, 6, 11, 12, 13, 15, 17, 18, 19, 20, 22, 25, 27, 28, 29, 32, 54, 61, 68, 69, 74, 77, 78, 86, 125, 151, 165, 172
Durrance, Tommy, 80
Dye, Pat, 54, 56, 134, 136, 137

E

Eagles, Philadelphia, 28, 80
East Carolina University, 19
Edge, Shayne, 134

Ellenson, Gene, 61, 62
Engelberg, Bugsy, 29, 30
Engle, Rip, 171
Erickson, Dennis, 150
Everett, Tre, 43, 79, 89, 98, 100, 109, 114, 116, 119, 129, 151, 157, 161, 180
Ewell, Keith, 33

F

Fain Richard, 42, 64
Fairbanks, Chuck, 30
Falcons, Atlanta, 11, 34
Fernandez, Bud, 108
Fleming, Cory, 129
Fleming, Mike, 65
Florida State University, 5, 12, 29, 38, 48, 69, 70, 75, 85, 86, 87, 90, 150, 151, 159, 160-167, 188, 194, 195, 196
Foley, Jeremy, 93, 189
Ford, Danny, 32, 78
49ers, San Francisco, 14
Fouts, Dan, 80
Fox, Brian, 48, 145, 146, 176, 177, 179
Franks, Carl, 29, 43, 76, 78, 135
Freedom Bowl, 15
Freeman, Reggie, 162
Frier, Matt, 164, 165

G

Gamblers, Houston, 163
Garfield, Charles, Dr., 4

Gator Bowl, 79
Gault, Willie, 28
Georgia Tech, 3, 25, 26, 27, 65, 66, 74, 165, 173, 196
Georgia, University of, 4, 38, 48, 51, 52, 57, 59-65, 75, 85, 128, 134, 141-147, 151, 179, 182, 188, 195
Glenn, Kevin, 134
Goff, Ray, 61, 143, 144
Goldsmith, Fred, 174
Graves, Marvin, 109, 110, 111
Graves, Ray, 79, 80, 196, 197
Greensboro (N.C.) Women's College, 171
Griese, Bob, 196
Grow, Monty, 47

H

Hairston, Jack, 53
Hall, Galen, 13, 52, 176
Hallman, Curly, 118
Harper, Jack, 193, 194, 195, 196
Harris, Sydney, Dr., 185
Hill Aubrey, 92, 109, 151, 157
Hines, Clarkston, 34
Hollingsworth, Gary, 41
Hollis, Charles, 95
Holmes, Oliver Wendell, 4
Houston, Harrison, 79, 88, 89, 90, 91, 107, 119, 121, 134, 140, 146, 162, 163, 166, 170
Houston, University of, 177

I

Ismail, Hesham, 85, 87, 153, 154
Ismail, Qadry, 109

J

Jackson, Terrell, 127, 129
Jackson, Willie, 70, 92, 99, 100, 109, 114, 116, 126, 130, 134, 138, 139, 145, 146, 162, 163, 170
Johnson, Antonio, 109
Jones, Cedric, 28

K

Keller, Greg, 88
Kelley, Mike, 173
Kelly, Andy, 45, 124, 127, 129
Kelly, Jim, 80
Kennedy, Larry, 85, 89, 127, 128, 129
Kentucky, University of, 48, 52, 54, 65-70, 95, 108, 128, 137, 145, 149-156, 159
Kinchen, Todd, 118
King, Bill, 44
King, Sam, 118
Kirkpatrick, Kirk, 40, 56, 67, 81
Knights, New Jersey, 73
Kramer, Roy, 149, 150, 154-155

L

Lacewell, Larry, 124, 127

Layton, Doug, 94, 95
Lee, Amp, 70, 163, 167
Ling, Betty, 81, 94
Lombardi, John, 65
Lombardi, Vince, 37
Louisiana State University, 85, 118, 119, 120, 121, 127, 128, 161
Lyle, Bob, 194, 195

M

MacDonald, Tom, 15
MacKay, Buddy, 66
Majors, Johnny, 49, 126
Marcum, Tim, 73, 76
Marino, Dan, 80
Maryland, University of, 3, 104
Matthews, Bill, 177
Matthews, Shane, 20, 21, 22, 38, 41, 42, 43, 47, 48, 54, 55, 56, 63, 67, 68, 88, 89, 90, 91, 92, 98, 100, 101, 106, 107, 109, 111, 114, 116, 119, 121, 126, 127, 129, 132, 134, 138, 139, 140, 144, 145, 146, 151, 152, 153, 155, 157, 161, 162, 163, 166, 169-170, 175-183, 196
McClendon, Ernie, 68
McClendon, Willie, 56, 92, 113, 134, 154
McCoy, Tony, 8, 83, 85, 75, 99, 105, 109, 115, 116, 120, 132, 160
McEwen, Tom, 136, 137

McGeorge, Rich, 77-78
McNabb, Dexter, 98, 100, 113
McRae, Charles, 45, 46
Melnyk, Steve, 173
Memphis State University, 69
Miami, University of, 12, 60, 69, 149-151, 160, 188, 193, 195
Michigan, University of, 13, 113, 114, 188
Mickell, Darren, 88, 128, 161, 167
Miles, Carlton, 91, 164, 168
Miller, Red, 30
Mills, Ernie, 41, 42, 55, 56, 67, 79, 147, 180
Mims, Chris, 45, 46
Mirer, Rick, 188
Mississippi State University, 85, 104, 108, 113, 114, 115, 116, 194
Missouri, University of, 196
Mobley, Dwayne, 81
Mora, Jim, 30
Morris, Kyle, 48, 176, 178, 179
Moss, Stan, 42
Murray, Mark, 64
Myles, Godfrey, 64, 67

N

NCAA, 3, 19, 22, 43, 52, 55, 60, 65, 68, 80, 86, 107, 125, 134, 188, 197
NFL, 11, 15, 28, 30, 31, 45, 46, 79, 88, 104, 143, 187
Nebraska, University of, 188

North Carolina State University, 78, 165, 196
North Carolina, University of, 12, 13, 29, 35, 69, 108, 165
Northern Illinois University, 108, 131, 132, 134
Northwestern University, 13, 32
Notre Dame, University of, 5, 150, 168, 170, 188, 196

O

O'Neal, Bill, 14, 15
O'Neal, Maston, 29, 30
Odom, Jerry, 64
Ohio State University, 27, 73, 85
Oklahoma State University, 38, 179
Ole Miss, 195
Oliver, Bill, 40
Orange Bowl, 150, 196

P

Packers, Green Bay, 37, 78
Pasqualoni, Paul, 104, 109
Patriots, New England, 28
Patton, George, General, 2
Paulk, Tim, 64, 85, 86, 134, 139, 168
Peace, Wayne, 194
Peach Bowl, 65
Penn State, 171
Perkins, Ray, 31

Pickens, Carl, 45, 47, 124, 127
Poole, Merrill, 142
Port, Chris, 34
Purdue University, 176, 196

R

Raisin Bowl, California, 88
Raleigh, Sir Walter, 5
Rauch, John, 76
Ray, Billy, 21, 22, 34
Reaves, John, 79-81, 135, 146,
176, 178
Rhett, Errict, 22, 47, 57, 63, 68,
77, 98, 100, 113-118, 129, 130,
134, 137-140, 145, 146, 152-
154, 156, 161, 166
Rice University, 12, 13, 174
Richardson, Huey, 64
Rodgers, Pepper, 25, 26, 27,
65, 74, 173
Rowell, Tony, 85, 87, 154, 165

S

SEC, 1, 7, 12, 37, 39, 43, 52, 53,
55, 59, 65, 66, 68, 69, 73, 75, 77,
79, 81, 85-87, 90, 93-95, 104,
108, 115-117, 128, 129, 134, 139,
142, 146, 149, 152, 153-156, 159,
165, 167, 168, 175, 179, 182,
187, 189, 193, 195, 197, 198
Sain, Tim, 108
Sally, Ron, 27
San Jose State University, 72,
88, 89, 90, 91

Sanders, Bob, 33, 42, 74
Schembechler, Bo, 113, 114,
115
Scott, Jim, 84
Sells, Jack, 123
Shaw, George Bernard, 1
Shea, Terry, 88
Showboats, Memphis, 173
Slayden, Steve, 21, 22
Sloan, Steve, 32, 74
Smith, Chuckie, 45, 46, 129
Smith, Emmitt, 186-187
Smith, Larry, 193
Smith, Lex, 176, 178
South Carolina, University of,
27, 29, 32
Southern Methodist
University, 193, 194
Speer, Del, 152, 164, 165
Spencer, Jimmy, 47
Speronis, Jamie, 81
Spurrier, J. Graham, Reverend,
5
Spurrier, Jerri, 72, 99, 135, 171-
174
Spurrier, Steve, 116, 132, 173,
174, 193-197
Stacey, Siran, 97
Stallings, Gene, 94
Stallions, Birmingham, 30, 78
Stanford University, 13
Stars, Philadelphia
(Baltimore), 25, 30, 31
Stowers, Rodney, 115
Strong, Charlie, 73, 76
Sugar Bowl, 5, 68, 86, 87, 137,

149, 150, 155, 168-170, 187, 188, 193-196
Sullivan, Alonzo, 97, 98, 100, 145, 146, 152, 153, 155, 157
Sullivan, Pat, 136
Syracuse University, 103-111, 113, 118

T

Tennessee, University of, 25, 28, 29, 32, 38, 45-49, 52, 53, 55, 56, 65, 73, 79, 85, 119, 123-131, 165, 188
Texas Christian University, 136
Texas Tech, 13, 15
Texas, University of, 12
Thomas, Harvey, 85, 162, 164, 167, 168
Trammell, Allen, 196
Travis, Larry, 25, 26
Tulane University, 26

U

USFL, 29, 30, 31, 76, 78, 173, 191

V

Vanderbilt University, 12
Veatch, Matt, 90
Vikings, Minnesota, 31
Virginia Tech, 29
Virginia, University of, 12, 13, 25, 27, 29, 32

W

Wake Forest University, 165
Walker, David, 19
Walker, Herschel, 182
Washington, University of, 15, 188
Weldon, Casey, 70, 161, 162, 163, 164, 167
White, Mark, 85, 87
White, Reggie, 28
White, Stan, 140
White, Will, 41, 47, 85, 98, 100, 139, 164
William and Mary, College of, 26
Williamson, Eddie, 27
Wilson, Barry, 31
Wilson, Red, 17, 27-29
Womack, Doug, 110
Wooden, John, 3
World Football League, 73, 81
Wynn, George, 146

Y

Young, Kurt, 66

Z

Zook, Denise, 73
Zook, Ron, 22, 73, 89, 123, 124
Zuberer, Bud, 34